*This book is practical, provocative and personal. It's well researched and joins a growing library of concerned researchers and authors who are disturbed by the very real impact and change that social media addiction and usage is creating in our world. The good news is that we can be in charge by becoming aware and following a different drum and Katie's book helps you to do that.*

Helena Holrick, Personal Progress Coach, *Helping You Shine.*

*Reading this book has been a pleasure from beginning to end. I immersed myself in this journey and came out feeling held, supported, and informed.*

*Katie guides us through the sometimes-tricky waters of today's digital landscape with expert insight, compassionate inquiry, and true grace. Through this book, she weaves together an elegant map to support us in honouring our energy, taking responsibility for how, why, and when we show up online, and implementing one of our most vital inner resources of this time: discernment. Thank you, Katie for this soul-nourishing gift, and for sharing your heart and wisdom with us.*

Lucy Anne Chard, Coach & Mentor for
Healers, Intuitives & Wayshowers.

*Given the current digital landscape and its impact on how we relate to each other and to ourselves both on and offline in the 21st century, such a book has never been more needed, or more perfectly timed. Through Katie's exploration, we have a fantastic opportunity to think about how to use social media, our devices and tech in more truly conscious, balanced, healthy and loving ways.*

Huw Mathias – Designer at
*Light Work Create.*

*The book we all need to read. Katie explores those uncomfortable questions about social media that need to be brought into the light, which we need to look at to create a well needed shift. She does so with grace, truth and authenticity. This book connects to the individual as well as the bigger picture and gets us to look at the root issues rather than glossing* over it. *Giving practical ideas to begin the process of change, for our long term wellness and wellbeing.*

Hannah Wallace, Model, Speaker, Podcaster *'Finding Grace'*.

*None of us are immune to the addictive and manipulative nature of social media, and sadly whether by design or by accident, many apps have ended up in this place. Kate's refreshingly honest book shows how we got here, what to do about it and where next – the potential future really is brighter and more human-centric, yea!*

Sue Farmer, Leadership Coach, Shamanic Healer, *Opportuniality*.

*Social media, urgh! My soul would sink at the prospect if it were not for the joy of all that Katie advocates. Community is all about 'comm-unity'. Communication that unites us. YYYEEESSS! Now this makes sense! Count your blessings not your followers. All of this sounds like my kind of social media 'strategy'. Yes Katie, I hear you. I'm in.*

Ryan James, Founder, Coach & Facilitator of *We Won't Die Wondering*.

*Katie is an acknowledged social media expert; in this readable and practical book she explores her mixed feelings about the impact and future of social media, the pressures to post and look good, how to survive, thrive and create an audience whilst remaining authentic. A great read for anyone wrestling with how to ethically build a social media presence.*

Dr. Phil Parker, PhD, *Lightning Process* Designer~Lecturer, London Met University~NLP author & trainer~ Mind-body connection and addictions expert.

*If you are even a tiny bit disillusioned about social media for business or personal reasons, this book helps you to make sense of why. Kdot shares wisdom and insight about why and how we got here, but also provides us with guidance on how to preserve our energy, how to be more conscious in our virtual worlds and to love it at the same time. As a fellow hippy business owner, I've always found it hard to break out of the way we've been 'taught' to do it and Katie's book lovingly confirms there is another way!*

Sarah Lloyd, PR & communications expert, author of *Connecting the Dots*.

*Katie Brockhurst shows real insight in calling out the toxic dark forces of social media - surveillance capitalism dressed up as a rat race for likes, clicks and sales. We need to urgently and radically transform the way we approach social media and the effect it has on our wellbeing and this book is a manifesto for positive change.*

Pete Lawrence, Founder of *Campfire Convention* and *The Big Chill Festival.*

*Katie always has her finger on the pulse. In this book she discusses the future of social media, with ethics, impact and health at the fore. The essence of the book poses the very relevant question: "How do we move forward into 2020 and beyond?" This is a visionary approach if I ever saw one, from someone who embodies Sacred Leadership from the inside out. Deep gratitude, Kdot.*

Henrietta Gothe-Ellis, Founder of *Sacred Leadership.*

*As we move into the 2020's this book is a must-read for all conscious business-owners who are using social media. Katie gives such a powerful overview of what's an ultra-fast-*

*moving landscape, as well as ideas about how to navigate this shape-shifting online world and look after ourselves at the same time. I feel uplifted and hopeful that the ways we use and engage with social media can create real change and bring a completely new energy to the way we connect online. Thank you SO much Katie for stepping forward to light the way!*

Nicola Humber, Author of *UNBOUND*.
Founder of *The Unbound Press*.

*I love Katie's message and how she has synthesised it all remains fascinating to me. I love how she is at the forefront of this thinking.*

Erin Ryan Mazcko, Employee
Experience Designer.

**Hey,**

Welcome to this wonderful book brought to you by That Guy's House Publishing.

At That Guy's House we believe in real and raw wellness books that inspire the reader from a place of authenticity and honesty.

This book has been carefully crafted by both the author and publisher so that it will bring you hope, inspiration and sensation of inner peace.

It is our hope that you thoroughly enjoy this book and pass it onto somebody who may also be in need of a glimpse into their own magnificence.

Have a wonderful day.

Love,

*Sean Patrick*

*That Guy.*

www.ThatGuysHouse.com

This edition is published by
That Guy's House in 2019

© Copyright 2019, Katie Brockhurst
All rights reserved.

No part of this publication may be reproduced,
stored, in a retrieval system, or transmitted, in
any form or by any means without permission
of the publisher.

www.ThatGuysHouse.com

# SOCIAL MEDIA FOR A
# NEW AGE

A Digital Self-Care Guide.

The next phase : 2020 & beyond

# KATIE BROCKHURST

# CONTENTS

# THE PROLOGUE

*I want to take you on a journey,*
*Through digital time and space...*
*To Social Media For A New Age,*
*Which is a kind and loving place,*
*Where we carefully consider,*
*What the Book of Face,*
*Is actually doing to us,*
*And the human race.*

As you begin to read this book, be it through paper pages, an e-reader, tablet or listening on your phone, imagine that I am waving to you now. Ethereally, digitally and spiritually, much like one of those photos in *The Daily Prophet*. They are all platforms, a communication tool for us to connect, share and meet through.

I'm Katie Brockhurst, also known as Kdot, the Social Media Angel. I have been working with social media for twenty years; my first foray was setting up a social network at university in 2000. Fascinated by the power of digital content and social media, I went on to co-produce and create a podcast which won Gold in the first ever 'Internet Programme' category at the *Sony Radio Academy Awards* in 2007 and set up my agency Kdot Online soon after. You can read more about my journey in my first book, which was shortlisted as a finalist at *The Business Book Awards* 2019. You can also read more about me at the back of this book.

I see our world and these various platforms we use to communicate becoming more magical and futuristic. Grids of connectivity where we share transmissions through our stories, content encoded with our energy, blending with each other more and more, as we ask: what is reality? We are moving differently now through time and space, part of a digital society and culture, managing many digital portals and identities. Time, energy and reality are more malleable than before.

In book one, I share how we are in the midst of a new age, a digital age, a pivotal point in our evolution. Yet this merge with technology in many ways is an experiment for and on the human race, with the latest data and insights only now revealing the longer term impacts digital life is having on our bodies, brains and wellbeing.

*It is hard to keep track of reality,*
*As we merge more deeply with technology.*
*Becoming more aware of what it's doing*
*to our psychology.*

In my twenty years of working with social media, I have come to see the many ways it can be both good and bad for us. For society, for democracy and culture, for our relationships and businesses. For our health, mind, body and spirit. This book is an account of what I see and feel happening in digital culture. I share about the importance of ethical social media in digital society, alongside ideas on how to manage our digital wellbeing, avoiding burnout whilst working in today's world.

> *Ethical social media users can steer conversations away from dark places and toward more productive and informative interaction. It is not simply a matter of 'be good to others': it is the ability to guide others and set standards that help, protect and encourage all sorts of voices.*

Source: University of Sydney; Dr Jonathon Hutchinson, Ethical Social Media MOOC.

My work has a liberal tone which embraces my personal and spiritual beliefs, considered 'New Age' by some. I like to call myself an 'Executive Hippy.' At the core it is ultimately about how we approach social media with a strategy of love, truth, kindness and self care.

If you are a returning reader, welcome back into my world and thank you for continuing to be open to how and what I share. If you are new, hello, it is good to have you here. Just as I see how we connect energetically with each other through social media content, we are also connecting through this book. If you enjoy it and it helps you, please find me on Instagram @ katiekdot_socialmediaangel and tell me about your experience with it. Tell your friends, write a review on Amazon or invite me to speak on your podcast or event. As an independent author, your comments, messages and support help me to continue on this path and reach people organically. Thank you.

This will read as a stand-alone book, as well as being part two in the series of *Social Media For A New Age* (so if you haven't read the first one, there is more to explore). With social media being such a fast-evolving entity, please forgive me if anything is already out of date; it is a huge topic and it moves so quickly. I have a lot of experience in working with social media, but in this day and age where social media is the new norm, that is no longer uncommon. It is a very different digital landscape to when I started my agency more than a decade ago.

I will be exploring our relationship to social media, particularly Facebook and its platforms, where I predominantly work with my clients. I also think Facebook Inc. has the biggest impact on digital society and our digital self, through the sheer power and influence of its platforms. I will get into the shadows and take a look at their owner and master, Mr. Mark Zuckerberg. *(Worlds first trans-humanist cyborg? Data from Star Trek's offspring? CIA operative?.... I joke (kinda). There are lots of interesting theories to be discovered on the internet!)* With plans to launch their own digital currency Libra, the imminent arrival of AR (augmented reality) and VR (virtual reality) platform Horizon, plus a paid partnership with news media companies, Facebook has been busy.

All of these aspects add up to something much bigger than we can currently understand or see with our physical eyes. Facebook's platforms are being used by the majority of online society to communicate on a daily basis, so I think we would benefit from caring more about what they are doing with us, our attention and our data.

As we look at the impact social media is having on our digital wellbeing, I will share my personal journey with you, as I realised that I was burnt out, disillusioned and addicted. I will be offering a *Social Media Angel Self Care Guide* at the end of this book and the ways in which I am approaching social media communication more consciously as we move into this next decade. I am bringing digital self-care to the forefront and centre, as we mature into the next phase, of *Social Media For A New Age.*

*There's no such thing as IRL because it is all REAL LIFE.*

Quote from technology psychologist Doreen Dodgen-Magee, in her brilliant book *'Deviced!'*

# #SOCIALMEDIAFORANEWAGE

This book was written in two months, in two sittings, six months apart. I didn't think I was going to finish it, but like a bolt out of the blue I received very clear guidance during a meditation on a full moon to continue and by the next full moon (the Beaver Moon no less), it was done. With the information so pertinent to this moment, it has been a quick turn around to release it for 2020, so please allow for any imperfections; indeed, please love it all the more for them, will you?

My confidence was knocked this year when a long-term client let me go. I had no drive to push or seek for work to replace the work I'd lost. People were contacting me, asking me to help manage platforms and market products, but instead of jumping on those leads, I would not follow up. It has been a weird and sometimes scary place to be in, but with my intuition guiding me, I knew deep down that I had to trust it, to trust *in* it and to trust it all.

I have not been enjoying social media as much lately. Being on it a lot for my work for so many years, I could see and feel a sense of disenchantment, of burnout, both individually and collectively.

Being on social media can feel very overwhelming day in and day out. Busy. Bustling. Some people you know, some you don't. Slide over an inspiring meme. Ooh look, a celebrity. Hop over some unsolicited advice. Side-step a preachy post. Get some advice on the moon phase. On business. On life. Ascension symptoms. Solar Flares. Then notice the ego is feeling something. Oh, it's comparison. A smidge of envy. A dash of despair. Oh there's someone or something that's upset me popping up just over there. And… Now I want those shoes… And that skirt… And to be on that dreamy looking holiday. Dammit.

Imagine all of that going on inside my head within a few moments of scrolling. Post after post, with the potential to spiral me into a personal *social media vortex of doom,* trying to grab my attention, tickling those emotional triggers. Post after post carrying an intention to get a reaction, a click, a Like or a sale. This is how we have been programmed to play, yes? Get Likes. Get follows. Get shared. Get engagement. Get comments. Get sales. Be seen. Be validated. That's the game, the gamification of social media, built into the system to get our attention, to get our data and ultimately our dollars.

Russell Brand recently shared something that speaks to this:

> *Is it possible for social media to become a place to share positivity and encourage kindness? Is that likely? What prevents that? Now we know that Facebook have run experiments in the past. Where they continually promoted comments that were negative on your Facebook feed. I think they did this in Australia. They could encourage purchase. They could encourage people towards purchasing. Now, I'm no sociologist as you know, but I think it's broadly accepted that by creating a state of negativity and inadequacy and inferiority, you can encourage people to consume.*

Source: YouTube; Russell Brand, *Dua Lipa - Is She Right About Online Toxic Abuse?*

This game of social media can affect our wellbeing, especially when we play everyday. Many of us playing it for money, for marketing, for work, for our businesses, for our dreams. Yet as creators and sharers, sometimes when we don't get those things- the Likes, the comments, the sales, the reach- we feel sad, unseen, unappreciated, unloved and unsuccessful on some level, which can play all sorts of havoc on our hearts. Do you feel this too?

*Social [media] affects my mental and emotional health, especially when I'm feeling wobbly or off balance; things can catch me off guard and I get sucked into the comparison trap. I've just had a two week total ban on social (apart from posting and then uninstalling immediately after!) And I'll have another total break this weekend because my mind needs the space! Love to you KDot! You're my social media rock star.*

Source: Instagram; comment from
Kathy Bell @kathybell

If we are active on social media, we are not immune from these feelings popping up somewhere inside ourselves when we hop on and off it, even if we are not fully conscious of it. We are not immune from feeling those moments when the social dopamine slot machine doesn't line up with the winning prize of Likes, comments or shares.

Being on social media so much for work was really starting to affect my nervous system. Scrolling my timeline was making my body tighten up and contract internally, as I would read posts and feel the energy behind them. Being energetically sensitive, I was picking up on so much, forgetting how overwhelming digital energy can be, like being out in a crowd.

One day mid-scroll, I saw a very vulnerable and intimate post about someone's drug addiction, relating it to a toxic sexual relationship. It was a true story, sexually graphic and emotive. The post ended with a call to action: 'Get the early bird special on my online course'. This quickly turned the post from a personal and vulnerable sharing to something else entirely. It left me feeling manipulated and angry. Someone else trying to get me to read a thing, sign up to a thing or buy a thing.

I get strong reactions to this kind of marketing and communication. It's visceral, I really feel it in my body and it isn't nice. I do understand why marketing has gone this way online and know of people working with coaches on their copy writing for ads and posts, where this is being taught.

I have so much compassion for everyone trying to 'make it' online right now; it is a confusing landscape. We need to share our stories, our vulnerabilities with each other and be truly seen by others, like Brené Brown, the author of *Daring Greatly* shares in her twenty years of research on the power of vulnerability. It is beautiful and powerful in the right context. We are wired for connection. Yet the connection we have created between vulnerability and marketing really rattles my cage and my nervous system. I don't think it is healthy for us to be served with these different kinds of energies, information or trauma stories in such an interruptive way throughout our day, in the name of marketing. Having better boundaries about what and where we share, thinking more carefully about what we are doing to each other energetically with our posts is something I would like to see happening more in *Social Media For A New Age: The Next Phase*.

We need communication that doesn't play into an old paradigm of persuasion and manipulation, and instead look at how to magnetise the right people to our words, our videos, our podcasts, our courses, our work in a more wholesome and less invasive way.

I don't have all the answers, but I am willing to try and unpick some of the bad habits and social conditioning that has been encouraged within social media marketing over recent years. It has become a massive market place full of promotion, advertising and attention-seeking. When you add in all the sponsored posts we see, every three to four in our timeline (I counted them this morning), there are a lot of diverse hooks and energies coming up and at us. We don't see what all of this is doing to us, every time we tap in.

*We zone it out,*
*We continue to scroll,*
*Energetically exhausting us all.*

> 'My friends and I are sick of being sold things all the time,' said Ms. Fisher, a student at University of South Florida with 1,342 Instagram followers. 'When you scroll through your Instagram feed, it's one sponsored post after another.'

Source: Wall Street Journal, *'Online Influencers Tell You What to Buy, Advertisers Wonder Who's Listening'* by Suzanne Kapner and Sharon Terlep.

I know a lot of my friends, clients and contemporaries are feeling this same sense of *enough!* The push, push, push of so much marketing and promotion feels relentless within these communication channels, particularly when it relates to sensitive topics around healing, mental health and wellbeing. It made me question social media as a whole, my role in it, where I want to go and how I earn a living. I needed to put myself on a time out, trusting in it as a cosmic redirection towards the *Social Media For A New Age* I started to pave with book one.

> *Excellent read. Informative, looking at social media from a totally different – and healthy - angle.*

Source: Wishing Shelf Book Awards finalist feedback; Male reader, aged 44 (praise for Social Media For A New Age 1).

This path is taking me into new realms within social media, where we begin expanding our awareness of what social media is and what it can do. Where we see it from both a collective, global view to an individual human perspective. The macro and the micro. What has unfolded throughout 2018-19 is just the beginning of what I'm sure will be an eye-opening decade ahead. As we approach what is hailed astrologically as the great conjunction of January 2020, I have to trust how I feel, and act on it.

> *All around the globe, astrologers are waiting with bated breath, for the BIGGEST conjunction of our lifetime – the meeting of these two giants, Pluto and Saturn, in*

*January 2020. Death meets Karma. The End meets the Timekeeper. They're ready to collapse an entire timeline, an entire era, and release it through the South Node of the Moon, the point of endings, releasing and purging. We are entering a new era – an age of light.*

Source: Facebook; Lilliana Letic, Astrologer & Shamanic Healer.

Managing fewer social media platforms has ultimately been a gift and it has given me a much-needed break from 'having' to be on multiple accounts for clients all the time. Inspired by Glastonbury Festival, I decided to take this as a fallow year, a year of rest and recovery, of research and development, as I turned forty and into a new age, a new decade of my own.

Reminding myself that time and space is a gift, not a punishment. It is amazing that even as free-thinking as I like to believe I am, how conditioned I still am into thinking that we are always meant to be on - on - on - earning, doing, posting, scrolling, spending, especially as a small business, as an entrepreneur. Remembering just how important rest is as part of that cycle, I have used this as a massive opportunity to watch and learn about my relationship with social media, my work, my life and technology. I have seen just how unhealthy my relationship to tech can be. As I write this I am still working on finding my balance. It will probably always be a work in progress. I want to use technology and social media in my life and my business, but not have it *be* my life. I'm sure many of you feel much the same.

I'm writing this for me, as much as for you.

*A sort of accidental, second manifesto.*

# PART ONE:

# DIGITAL SOCIETY
# AND THE DIGITAL SELF

# CHAPTER ONE:

# A BAD YEAR
# FOR FACEBOOK?

*Billions of users,*
*And dollars too.*
*Zuck's been riding high*
*But does he really know what to do?*
*From his dorm room,*
*To the boardroom,*
*To everyones pocket,*
*Where we consume.*
*He thought he was on a roll...*
*But are things now out of control?*

When the Cambridge Analytica scandal broke in March 2018, it revealed how the information we give to Facebook was being used to politically profile users, with the intention to persuade voters. This is particularly relevant to the outcomes of the Presidential election in the USA in 2016 and the Brexit referendum in the UK. The winning parties in both cases were spending money on Facebook advertising, with Cambridge Analytica working on the digital campaigns.

I have learned so much more about Facebook since then, information which has rocked my faith in this digital metropolis, in the digital space we have all moved into. A place where I have spent the last decade, dedicated to helping people build platforms, using it to grow their businesses and reach more people. I feel that I naively placed my trust, as many of us have, in Facebook Inc. They appear to be very out of favour with the mainstream media and have been making a lot of headlines, and trust in the company is at an all-time low.

Having watched Mark Zuckerberg speak to Congress about Facebooks new digital currency Libra, where he was questioned on a number of topics relating to the power both he and Facebook have, I am concerned. I wonder who is he working with and if he really knows what he is doing.

> *Congress is grilling him about how the social media network he created to keep tabs on the relationship status of his crush is facilitating the downfall of Western civilisation.*

Source: *Rolling Stone Magazine: Alexandria Ocasio-Cortez Exposed Mark Zuckerberg and Facebook : Facebook isn't only tolerating disinformation in political advertisements, it's facilitating it,* by Ryan Bort.

To explore this further, I want to share an interesting exchange between Mark Zuckerberg and New York district congresswoman Alexandria Ocasio-Cortez. If you haven't already seen it, it is worth watching or reading. It was one of the most reported on questions he was asked during the roughly six hour hearing. I love how she begins:

> *Mr Zuckerberg, I think you of all people can appreciate using a person's past behaviour in order to determine, make decisions or predict people's future behaviour, and in order for us to make decisions about Libra I think we need to dig into your past behaviour and Facebook's past behaviour with respect to our democracy.*

She continues by asking about their new policy on advertising for politicians, an advertising policy that was changed soon after Zuckerberg had a closed-door meeting with President Trump.

> *Ocasio-Cortez: Could I run ads on Facebook targeting Republicans in primaries saying that they voted for the Green New Deal? If you're not fact-checking political advertisements... I'm just trying to understand the bounds of what is fair game.*

> *Zuckerberg: Congresswoman, I don't know the answer to that off the top of my head.*

> *Ocasio-Cortez: So you don't know if I'll be able to do that?*

> *Zuckerberg: I think probably.*

> *Ocasio-Cortez: Do you see a potential problem here with a complete lack of fact-checking on political advertisements?*

> *Zuckerberg: Congresswoman, I think lying is bad. I think if you were to run an ad that had a lie, that would be bad. That's different from it being... from it... in our position the right thing to do to prevent, uhh, your*

*constituents or people in an election from seeing that you had lied...*

*Ocasio-Cortez: So you won't take down lies or you will take down lies? It's a pretty simple yes or no?*

*Zuckerberg: Congresswoman, in most cases, in a democracy, I believe people should be able to see for themselves what politicians they may or may not vote for are saying and judge their character for themselves.*

*Ocasio-Cortez: So you won't take them down? You may flag that it's wrong, but you won't take it down?*

*Zuckerberg: Congresswoman, it depends on the context that it shows up... organic posts... ads...*

Source: Live video streamed from Capitol Hill, October 23, 2019 in Washington, DC.

# Personalised Persuasion and Propaganda.

I wanted to understand how these targeted political posts and ads worked. I wanted to know how they have been manipulating us, so I could protect myself better by being more aware of what is going on in our newsfeeds and with our data. Because if Cambridge Analytica weren't doing it anymore (they claimed for bankruptcy soon after the scandal), you can bet your bottom dollar that someone else probably will be and it will have gone dark. Somewhere out there, it is likely that governments, politicians or companies are using this kind of advanced targeting through social media. It will not have gone away; it's too powerful.

In *The Great Hack*, a documentary on Netflix about how our data is being used in this way, Brittany Kaiser, a whistle blower who worked at Cambridge Analytica says:

> *Psychographics should be considered weapons grade communications tactics.*

Source: Netflix; *The Great Hack,* Brittany Kaiser

Does Facebook know this? You can make up your own mind about that.

During my research I also learned that profiles and accounts weren't always using fake news, as I assumed, to change our thinking. Instead content was being created with the intention to manipulate our emotions, either one way or the other, using opposing opinions.

> *These accounts don't change what you think, but exaggerate what you feel. This network wasn't trying to change your mind, it was trying to confirm it. To make you even surer that you are right, and make you angrier with the people who are wrong. The messages were poles apart, and all of it was calculated to provoke exactly the same response: outrage. This strategy, a similar one to those uncovered on Twitter in the past, is all about inhabiting both ends of the political spectrum, and to pull them further and further, angrier and angrier apart.*

Source: Wired; *"It's still ridiculously easy to manipulate Facebook with anger".*

As I watched *The Great Hack* on Netflix my mouth fell open when I learned about Cambridge Analytica's approach to political campaigns. Cambridge Analytica called themselves 'a behaviour change agency', and it appeared that the people in charge at Facebook *were aware* of what they were doing, as they were working directly with their advertising teams.

In the run up to the 2020 Presidential campaign it is possible that our data will be targeted in even more sophisticated ways to 'change behaviour'. It does not appear like Facebook is trying to make this any better at this point. If anything, like Alexandria Ocasio-Cortez suggested when she questioned Zuck in congress, he is saying it is OK for politicians to lie on their platforms. Katie Harbath, Public Policy Director for Global Elections at Facebook wrote this in a letter to Joe Biden's Campaign, which was reported by the New York Times, after they complained about a sponsored post by Trump:

> *Our approach is grounded in Facebook's fundamental belief in free expression, respect for the democratic process, and the belief that, in mature democracies with a free press, political speech is already arguably the most scrutinised speech there is. Thus, when a politician speaks or makes an ad, we do not send it to third party fact checkers.*

Source: New York Times; *Facebook's Hands-Off Approach to Political Speech Gets Impeachment Test'* by Cecilia Kang.

Politicians have been speaking up about it. Elizabeth Warren, the Massachusetts senator and Democratic presidential candidate, invested in a series of Facebook ads that targeted both Donald Trump and Mark Zuckerberg with intentionally false information, as a way to make her point.

> *Facebook changed their ads policy to allow politicians to run ads with known lies—explicitly turning the platform into a disinformation-for-profit machine. This week, we decided to see just how far it goes. We intentionally made a Facebook ad with false claims and submitted it to Facebook's ad platform to see if it'd be approved. It got approved quickly and the ad is now running on Facebook. Take a look.*

Source: Senator Elizabeth Warren @ewarren (on Twitter).

**Elizabeth Warren**
Sponsored · Paid for by **Warren for President**

Breaking news: Mark Zuckerberg and Facebook just endorsed Donald Trump for re-election.

You're probably shocked, and you might be thinking, "how could this possibly be true?"

Well, it's not. (Sorry.) But what Zuckerberg *has* done is given Donald Trump free rein to lie on his platform -- and then to pay Facebook gobs of money to push out their lies to American voters.

If Trump tries to lie in a TV ad, most networks will refuse to air it. But Facebook just cashes Trump's checks.

Facebook already helped elect Donald Trump once. Now, they're deliberately allowing a candidate to intentionally lie to the American people. It's time to hold Mark Zuckerberg accountable—add your name if you agree.

**Mark Zuckerberg just endorsed Donald Trump**
It's time to break up our biggest tech companies like Amazon, Google, and Facebook.
MY.ELIZABETHWARREN.COM

Sign Up

See Ad Details

This issue has been gaining momentum while I have been writing, with a letter leaked from over 250 staff at Facebook HQ demanding Zuckerberg change his position on this. This gives us some hope.

*'Free speech and paid speech are not the same thing,' the letter reads, according to a copy of it published by the NYT. 'Misinformation affects us all. Our current policies on fact checking people in political office, or those running for office, are a threat to what FB stands for. We strongly object to this policy as it stands. It doesn't protect voices, but instead allows politicians to weaponise our platform by targeting people who believe that content posted by political figures is trustworthy.'*

Source: Business Insider; *Hundreds of Facebook employees call on Mark Zuckerberg to change the social network's controversial rules on political ads,* by Rob Price.

Twitter have since responded to the controversy surrounding political adverts with CEO Jack Dorsey making the decision to ban them altogether. I expect this ethical social media question around political advertising is likely to keep making the headlines.

*'It's not just about one election, it's about so many of the choices that we're facing in society right now,' Clinton reportedly said about the current moment. 'The use of our data to manipulate us, to make money off of*

*us, is really one of the cardinal challenges we face ... this is our information, but people seem to forget that they should demand to own it.'*

Source: CNET; Hillary Clinton: *Zuckerberg should 'pay a price' for hurting democracy. Clinton speaks out about social media and the 'war on truth,'* by CNET News Staff.

We will have to see what happens as we roll through 2020 and beyond.

As David Carroll, an associate professor of media design who filed a formal complaint against Cambridge Analytica, in *The Great Hack* says,

*Our dignity as humans is at stake.*

Source: Netflix; *The Great Hack,* David Carroll.

## Digital Gangsters

In 2018-19 the UK Governments Digital, Culture, Media and Sport select committee had a 18-month investigation into disinformation and fake news where they described Facebook in their final report as a 'digital gangster'.

> *Facebook behaves like a digital gangster. It considers itself to be 'ahead of and beyond the law'. It 'misled' parliament. It gave statements that were 'not true'. Its CEO, Mark Zuckerberg, has treated British lawmakers with 'contempt'. It has pursued a 'deliberate' strategy to deceive Parliament.*

Source: The Guardian newspaper, *A digital gangster destroying democracy: the damning verdict on Facebook,* by Carole Cadwalladr.

Damian Collins, the committee's chairman, also warns us in the report:

> *Democracy is at risk from the malicious and relentless targeting of citizens with disinformation and personalised 'dark adverts' from unidentifiable sources, delivered through the major social media platforms we use every day.*

It seems this is a good time to be asking if Mark Zuckerberg should have so much control and if it is time for regulation.

Zuck released an article about his vision - *A Privacy Focussed Vision for Social Networking*- where he writes about 'bad things' on the network...

> *There are real safety concerns to address before we can implement end-to-end encryption across all of our messaging services. Encryption is a powerful tool for privacy, but that includes the privacy of people doing bad things.*

> *When billions of people use a service to connect, some of them are going to misuse it for truly terrible things like child exploitation, terrorism, and extortion. We are working to improve our ability to identify and stop bad actors across our apps by detecting patterns of activity or through other means, even when we can't see the content of the messages, and we will continue to invest in this work.*

While it seems he is addressing some of the issues relating to the problems we find on social media, I feel that he isn't owning mistakes Facebook has made. He is completely by-passing how Facebook itself uses and sells our data to advertisers, politicians and corporations on the platform.

> *My focus for the last couple of years has been understanding and addressing the biggest challenges facing Facebook. This means taking positions on important issues concerning the future of the internet. In this note, I'll outline our vision and principles around building a privacy-focused messaging and social networking platform. There's a lot to do here, and we're committed to working openly and consulting with experts across society as we develop this.*

Source: Facebook; Mark Zuckerberg; March 7th 2019.

# Can We Trust the Zuck?

Facebook, and therefore Mark Zuckerberg, has great power and can influence billions of people worldwide, without our being aware of it.

At the time of writing this Zuck is worth c. $62.3 billion dollars (get your Austin Powers pinky out for that one) and is the world's third richest person. Someone give him a cat to stroke. [Searches internet for meme of Zuck stroking a cat, Bond villain style. Reddit gives me this. I do hope the picture isn't copyrighted. It is too good not to share.]

Posted by u/tywood2024 1 year ago

15 Mark Zuckerberg crushes poor cat in his high school years circa 1991

1991

Creating Facebook at just nineteen years old, he didn't finish his degree and he hasn't had any experience working anywhere else. He has been repeatedly asked by shareholders to step down from his role as Chief Executive, but he seemingly will not budge.

In a leaked audio from an internal Facebook team meeting this year, Zuckerberg is heard to say;

> *'So one of the things that I've been lucky about in building this company is, you know, I kind of have voting control of the company, and that's something I focused on early on,' Zuckerberg — told employees. 'And it was important because, without that, there were several points where I would've been fired.'*

Source: Business Insider article *Zuckerberg told employees that he would have been fired several times over if it weren't for his total control of Facebook.*

Internal grumblings at Facebook HQ have made it into the papers with a number of high profile people leaving the company due to disagreements with him and his team. The founders of both Instagram and WhatsApp left because they didn't agree with the direction Mark wanted to take with those digital properties and data. I wonder exactly why they left. Any reports and articles I have read and researched are unsurprisingly vague on the issues.

> *Zuckerberg says that Facebook can do better. But as someone who has covered this company for most of its life, I truly don't believe he's capable of change. If anything, Zuckerberg's 'pivot' is just a way for Facebook to monopolize another market and keep the cash flowing.*

Source: Vanity Fair: *THE FALSE PROMISE OF MARK ZUCKERBERG'S COME-TO-JESUS MANIFESTO,* by Nick Bilton.

I am keen to ask the Inner Unicorn Questions we should all be asking of

Facebook Inc: what is it is doing to the world through the ownership of Messenger, WhatsApp and Instagram? It impacts many of our day-to-day lives. It is a place where many of us run our businesses, communicate with others and spend many hours a day investing time and energy into, consciously or otherwise.

## Profits over People?

Amongst all of the scrutiny, Facebook continue to report record profits.

> *Despite the scandals and subsequent #DeleteFacebook campaign, Facebook posted record profits just before its 15th anniversary, an equivalent of $7.37 from each of its 2.32 billion users.*

Source: istock / Independent Newspaper.

Individually we are worth relatively little, but *en masse* we are worth a lot.

I hear of people turning away from Facebook or that they want to do so, but at this point it is not enough to make an impact.

Interestingly on March 13th, 2019, (in the midst of a Mercury retrograde for my astrology fans reading) Facebook Inc suffered one of its biggest outages to date. Its services across Facebook, Messenger, Instagram and WhatsApp were inaccessible for up to fourteen hours worldwide. During this down time I noticed what people did and where they went. A lot of people went to Twitter to ask what was going on with Facebook.

Aren't we funny, hive minded humans? We want to be connected, all the time, on some level, collectively. Facebook is where we do that. I don't know if I see that being replicated anywhere else, but we shall see. But when we have one company, one organisation who owns the main platforms used by the majority of a global online society, we really have given them a great amount of power.

Over the past fifteen years, many of us have put our golden eggs in Mark Zuckerberg's social media basket.

> *Look at what happens when we let one company control everything. Facebook is down which means Instagram and FB Workplace (where I communicate with my team & clients) are down. I figured this could happen eventually but it's extremely crippling to be part of this monopoly.*

Source: Twitter; Rebecca Brooker @beckybrooker

It is a basket that might break. It is a basket that has holes leaking our data. It is basket we can't fully trust. We need to decide on an individual and collective level how okay we are with that. If we are okay giving our time, our content, our energy and our advertising budget to them. If the pros outweigh the cons.

I've been supporting *The Campfire Convention*, an alternative social network. Something different, no algorithms or data collection, with a proposed profit-share system. A platform for social change, run by the people for the people. But it is no easy feat. Relying on volunteers and good will, founder Pete Lawrence, who was inspired by a forum he ran for the Big Chill Festival and what they achieved there, finds it ironic how much they have to use Facebook to communicate about the Campfire.

Facebook have more money than we can shake a stick at in terms of research, development and manpower. This makes it tough to compete, and if competition does arise, Zuck often tries to buy it. It is not a tool I necessarily want to turn my back on, not yet…

In a recent rebrand, FACEBOOK is trying to reinvent itself across Instagram, Facebook and Whatsapp, with this quote in the Guardian bringing a wry smile to my face:

> *The rebrand has prompted general eye-rolling – the AV Club's Allison Shoemaker points out that even peppering the logo*

*with unicorns would not save the company's image. But that won't stop marketing teams from trying.*

Source: The Guardian, *Facebook rebrands as FACEBOOK: can capital letters save a toxic brand?* by Matthew Cantor.

FACEBOOK is convenient. We can't blame it all on them. It's there, it's 'free', everyone is on it and it is easy and fun to use. I love the way it connects us to each other. It is something I use in so many ways. I often turn a blind eye to its shadow sides, but I have to start to draw lines and think more creatively about how I use it for good, how to be the light from the inside. And to be mindful of its quest for power and domination of all things digital. For example if Libra, FACEBOOK's proposed digital currency happens, I will do my best to resist using that service if I can.

*Most other cryptocurrencies are basically investment schemes. Libra is an effort to change the entire currency of the world. Facebook wants you to buy stuff with Libra and to send money to people with Libra.*

Source: Gzero Media: *Takeaway from Mark Zuckerberg Testimony on Capitol Hill.*

Why does this concern me? Ultimately because I think Mark Zuckerberg values profit over people.

And those people, that's us.

> *During his testimony before the House of Financial Services Committee, Rep. Roger Williams, R-Texas, asked the 35-year-old billionaire whether he's a capitalist or a socialist:*
>
> *'Congressman,' Zuckerberg said, suppressing a laugh, 'I would definitely consider myself a capitalist.'*

Source: Fox News.

# INNER UNICORN QUESTION TIME

- *Does Mark Zuckerberg know what is best for the future of the internet?*

- *If we want to have a say in the future of social media how can we be more actively engaged in the process?*

- *If Facebook Inc is out of alignment with our own personal morals and ethics, will we look elsewhere and into other options to communicate and connect?*

*Where there is light, there
must be shadow, where there
is shadow there must be light.
There is no shadow without light
and no light without shadow…*

Source: Good Reads; quote by Haruki Murakami.

# #SOCIALMEDIAFORANEWAGE

# CHAPTER TWO:

# THE SHADOW SIDE TO SOCIAL MEDIA

*This addiction is an affliction,*
*Programmed into us by their system.*
*Yet addiction by design,*
*Doesn't appear to be a crime.*
*Getting 'users' hooked like it's a lifeline,*
*Harvesting our energy, data and time...*
*Just so they can make more dime.*
*I want to take back what's mine.*

I am addicted to social media.

The itch to pick it up even though I only picked it up a few minutes ago. The tightness in my tummy, the fluttering in my stomach, the anticipation as the app opens up and as the screen refreshes its 'feed'. The butterflies as I await results; be it Likes, comments, messages, new content, news, connection, valuation, appreciation. Hunting for that feeling, that sensation, as I mindlessly hop from app to app, email to Facebook, Instagram to Messenger, Whatsapp to LinkedIn, Twitter, News or YouTube... Coming round to the reality that I'm hunched over a small bright rectangle, noticing I'm lost in an endless scroll, forgetting what I had come on to check, or do. Time lost, energy drained. Cross with myself for doing it again.

Learning that I was hooked on my own chemical reaction to social media was a big thing for me. Finding out that being on social media is producing dopamine, which is lighting up my system in all sorts of different ways. In similar ways to drugs like cocaine, alcohol and nicotine. It started to make more sense as to why my body would crave this 'hit', and the instinct to go hunting for it, when in need of a lift, even though this information has been sensationalised by the media somewhat.

> *What drugs release dopamine in the brain? Research has shown that the drugs most commonly abused by humans (including opiates, alcohol, nicotine, amphetamines, and cocaine) create a neuro-chemical reaction that significantly increases the amount of dopamine that is released by neurons in the brain's reward centre.*

Source: Hazledon Betty Ford Foundation: *Drug Abuse, Dopamine, and the Brain's Reward System.*

In my twenties I loved to rave with my friends at the weekends, indulging in lots of dopamine one way or another and I think I have some tendencies towards addiction. I have made sacrifices and lost some friends in putting those habits behind me. It concerns me now that I recognise my addiction to social media and the effects that it is having on my wellbeing and I wonder how this will affect my business.

I am not an expert on the science behind this, but from the research I have done I have come to understand that dopamine is not all bad. It can help with depression, with memory, with excitement and motivation. It can help us process pain and can help us to be more creative. But too much of it is also linked to addictive and repetitive behaviour, attention disorders and mental health conditions.

In response to this, I started to take measures to cut back on my device and social media usage, taking note of how it feels when I do. Looking at when I use my phone the most and when I use my phone the least. What drives those behaviours and what it feels like in my body. Looking for what gets me to want to pick up my phone; how long I spend on it and why.

Addictions and shadows are things we often can't see, or we ignore, because they are in a blind spot. It's uncomfortable to give some things up. Looking at our shadows can be scary and painful. This seems to be human nature. I doubt there is a human alive who *doesn't* have something in their life which this relates to. I don't believe any of us are perfect, ever will be or would want to be perfect. Our imperfections are beautiful, but when it is hurting ourselves or others, then being honest about it can be a first step to making things better.

Maybe Facebook can't see their own shadows, in order to own them. Maybe they don't want to. Addictive design appears to be common practice in Silicon Valley, so they may not even think they are doing anything wrong in the way it was designed. It makes the company money, therefore it is okay. They are opportunists; they didn't necessarily foresee what it would do.

The way Facebook has handled the issues of the past year has been interesting. I remember watching when Channel 4 news were covering the Cambridge Analytica scandal: the Facebook HQ in London had gone into lockdown. The whole building was locked and the lights were off. Live on the six o'clock news, the reporter was knocking on their big glass doors while staff hid inside pretending no-one was there. This felt like a symbol of them being in the dark, not able to face up to the truth of the situation or their mistakes, choosing instead to stay hidden from their own shadow.

But they say the wound is where the light gets in, so maybe there is hope for Facebook yet.

There is a movement in tech valley highlighting these issues, with *The Centre of Humane Technology* at the forefront.

> *Today's tech platforms are caught in a race to the bottom of the brain stem to extract human attention. It's a race we're all losing.*

*The result: addiction, social isolation, outrage, misinformation, and political polarisation—all part of one interconnected system called human downgrading that poses an existential threat to humanity. Our mission is to reverse human downgrading by realigning technology with our humanity.*

Source: Centre of Humane Technology - humanetech. com

Nir Eyal, author of the book *Hooked - How to Build Habit-Forming Products* ironically got hooked on such products himself and has just released his next book *Indistractable: How to Control Your Attention and Choose Your Life.*

He writes:

*We can take steps right now to retrain and regain our brains. To be blunt, what other choice do we have? We don't have time to wait for regulators to do something and if you hold your breath waiting for corporations to make their products less distracting, well you're going to pass out.*

Source: *Indistractable; How to Control Your Attention and Choose Your Life*, by Nir Eyal with Julie Li.

As a human (unicorn) being on this planet, I understand how we can all make mistakes; it is how we handle things once we are aware of the issues that I think matters the most. As I understand it, our response to a situation either clears or continues the karma.

It got me thinking, if Facebook was a family member or a friend- and lets face it, we spend as much time, if not more with our devices these days as we do with some of our closest people - can we forgive, forget and move on?

By looking at the shadow sides to social media, not only for myself but for all of us and for Facebook itself, I hope to be part of our healing. I want to help clear the energy, get the digital sage out, roll our sleeves up, clean up, move forwards and start a new chapter, a new age.

Social media and digital technology is not all bad, but I want to be aware of the pitfalls so I can kick my bad habits and use it that much more effectively.

This requires some commitment and sometimes some tough love. It is so easy to get away with bad digital habits. I have been reading *Digital Minimalism* by Cal Newport; he recommends taking a full 30-day break before reintroducing certain technologies and social media back into your life.

In his book, I discovered how the main social networks and mobile app builders had actively employed companies and consultants (including consultants from casinos and gambling houses) to find the best ways to get us addicted to their apps. They worked to find the best ways to create that addictive dopamine hit with 'addictive design' and 'persuasive technology'.

That fluttering in my stomach, the sense of anticipation I felt when I was opening up my apps or app-hopping, that physical reaction was cultivated, encouraged and programmed into my nervous system. The reaction was made stronger and stronger over time due to the repetitive nature of it. Each time I open up my phone, this action is strengthening the neural pathway and re-igniting the release of dopamine or feel good chemicals. My body over time is changing, no longer producing these chemicals naturally, instead leaving social media to do it for me. I learned this from scientifically-minded shamanic healer and business leadership coach, Sue Farmer, who I have been collaborating and working with for many years. We have a podcast episode called *Are You Addicted To Picking Up Your Phone* discussing this, which you can find on iTunes.

> *'A movement to be "post-digital" will emerge in 2020,' Mr. Fogg wrote last month. 'We will start to realise that being chained to your mobile phone is a low-status behaviour, similar to smoking.'*

Source: The New York Times, *Addicted to Screens? That's Really a You Problem* by Nellie Bowles.

Maybe Facebook and company didn't really think about what they were doing to us long-term by getting us all hooked. But with a reported big $3 billion plus investment into virtual reality and new platform Horizon, I hope they are being careful and consulting with psychologists to see what impact this is having or may have on our brains. As more studies start to emerge it is important we consider the risks.

> *A small-yet-significant study involving 47 healthy pre-school children between 3-5 years (27 girls & 20 boys) found structural differences in their brains caused by screen-based media.*

*Think: iPhones, computers, iPads, etc*

*The children exposed to more screen time had lower structural integrity of white matter tracts in their brain.*

*White matter tracts are VERY important - they support language & other developing literacy skills, including imagery & executive function + mental control & self-regulation.*

*Researchers can't yet definitively determine whether screen time = long-term neuro-developmental risks, but they do strongly urge parents adhere to the American Academy of Paediatrics screen-based recommendations.*

Source: Instagram; Danielle Shine @ChefShine (who I love and trust and who checks her sources and science.)

# Addictive by Design

Tristan Harris is the man behind *The Centre for Humane Technology*. In an interview by CNN Business, *How tech companies are addressing screen addiction* journalist Lisa Ling asks Harris:

> *So this compulsiveness that we feel when we look at our devices… You're saying thats by design?*

Harris replies:

> *Behind the screen are a hundred, in some cases a thousand engineers who go to work every single day, and their job is to figure out 'how can I keep you hooked,' using it for as long as possible, as frequently as possible and to make sure you come back tomorrow.*

To reiterate this, Sean Parker, the founding President of Facebook spoke at an event in 2017 about the 'attention engineering' adopted by his former company.

> *The thought process that went into building these applications, Facebook being the first of them,…was all about: 'How do we consume as much of your time and conscious attention as possible?' And that means that we need to sort of give you a little dopamine*

*hit every once in a while, because someone liked or commented on a photo or post or whatever.*

Source: *Digital Minimalism* by Cal Newport.

When I reach for my phone I now know to think *oh hiiiii little Like (aka dopamine) hunter.* I talk to this part of myself and I ask her what she is looking for when she is on the hunt. She's often looking for connection, approval and validation.

*The Opposite of Addiction is Connection. New addiction research brings surprising discoveries.*

Source: Psychology Today.

My social media addiction is at its most active when I am by myself for long periods of time. As someone who has been single for much of the past decade, living alone, working alone and often travelling alone, I have periods of time where much of my connection to my friends is through my mobile device and social media. This unbeknownst to me has created an addiction that I am now actively needing to manage and which causes me some concern, considering it is also directly linked to my work.

*And if social media addiction does exist, it would be a type of internet addiction – and that is a classified disorder. In 2011, Daria Kuss and Mark Griffiths from Nottingham Trent University in the UK have analysed 43 previous studies on the matter, and conclude that social media addiction is a mental health problem that 'may' require professional treatment. They found that excessive usage was linked to relationship problems, worse academic achievement and less participation in offline communities, and found that those who could be more vulnerable to a social media addiction include those dependent on alcohol, the highly extroverted, and those who use social media to compensate for fewer ties in real life.*

Source: BBC.com *Is Social Media Bad for You?* by Jessica Brown.

My mobile does make it a lot easier to not have to go out and meet people, especially when I am travelling, because my people are in my pocket. The truth is, sometimes I don't want to meet and hang out with people all the time. I want that alone time. I enjoy being in retreat mode, where I can create, concentrate and cultivate. Yet the urge to reach for the phone and see which of the people I love or am connected to have sent me a message, liked a message, left a comment can be much stronger when I don't have physical interaction with others.

I have access to my soul tribe across the world who have gravitated into my life naturally, both through being out in the world and through being online, which I see as a good thing. However it does enable me to go into hermit mode and I have noticed how I can hide out for quite long periods of time, longer than I would without my device. I find myself lost in an endless scroll and think, *What am I doing?! Get out of the house right now!* But I don't. I feel nervous or afraid to go out, especially at night by myself, and more so as I get older. I choose instead to pacify myself with social media, YouTube, Netflix etc.

As I talk a lot about in book one, there are so many positives we get from social media, but those positives do not cancel out the negatives I now see. They co-exist. The Like-hunting and constant checking is not a good thing for me. It can become a nervous tic at times and it can actually make me feel physically nauseous when I pick my phone up for what feels like the 50 millionth time that day.

By researching and writing about where I am out of balance, by saying the truth of these things out loud for this chapter and by becoming more aware of it, this work is helping me to heal it.

I decided to get more informed. As well as reading books on the topic, I have taken a *Digital Wellbeing* course created by the University of York. They share:

> *In a nutshell, when it comes to mental wellbeing and mental health, digital media is like a gust of air; it can fuel as much as blow out a fire.*

Source: FutureLearn; Digital Wellbeing Course by the University of York. Author Lina Gega.

Some of the best ways I have found to stop myself from checking or relying on my phone so much is to switch the phone into airplane mode or to put it in another room and give myself time with activities that don't involve a screen. Spending time with my cat Crystal or sitting in the garden, leaving the phone inside sound like such simple things, but it is crazy how much my phone was always coming along for the ride and then distracting me.

Reading a book with my phone off. Learning a musical instrument. (I'm learning to play the

Kalimba, a small handheld instrument, at the moment.) Going for a walk without my phone. Or calling up a friend and asking to hang out in person. Making sure my phone is always in my bag on silent mode and not given attention when with people. Simple but effective.

> *Studies of conversation both in the laboratory and in natural settings show that when two people are talking, the mere presence of a phone on a table between them or in the periphery of their vision changes both what they talk about and the degree of connection they feel. People keep the conversation on topics where they won't mind being interrupted. They don't feel as invested in each other. Even a silent phone disconnects us.*

Source: New York Times: Opinion; *Stop Googling. Let's Talk* by Sherry Turkle (who has been studying the psychology of online connectivity for more than 30 years).

Our mobile device is so many things: our safety net (phone), memories (camera), access to all the information in the world (Google), our navigation (maps), our friends (Whatsapp), a currency converter, time buddy, calculator, etc. The list goes on and on…

Having the phone so close all the time also means having the dopamine hit and addiction of social media available too. It is difficult to remove social media from the mix without deleting the apps from the phone. I also tell myself social media is important because it's my work, which is true. This has stopped me from removing the Facebook and Instagram apps, although I know if I removed them my usage would drop massively and my addiction would have some time to detox. Maybe that is the next step for me, but I know it feels uncomfortable. My device is such a support tool in living life on my own, and I worry that I would feel lost and alone without it. It is empowering and it is connective. But perhaps deleting these apps is an experiment I really need to try in order to strengthen my wellbeing and lessen social media's power over my mental health.

It is a double edged sword. In *Digital Minimalism - On Living Better with Less Technology,* Cal Newport recommends instead of taking time to declutter our technologies to instead:

> *...just go for a rapid transformation, by having a break from all 'optional technologies' for 30 days, using the time to rediscover activities and behaviours you enjoy outside of tech,*

*before reintroducing the optional tech and deciding what value it serves in your life.*

I recommend his book if you are wanting to learn and understand ways to liberate from technology overload. Another book that is currently blowing my mind on this topic of digital mindfulness and balance is by Dr Doreen Dodgen-Magee, a psychologist with 25 years of experience working with people and their relationship to technology. *Deviced! Balancing Life and Technology in a Digital World* is lighting me up, calming me down and healing my digital imbalances with all that she shares. We have a collaboration brewing in the ethers thanks to Instagram, reminding me just how good social media can be and that total abstinence is not the answer.

Finding a new balanced way forward has to be my future. But oh, how some of what she writes hits some tender spots for me.

> *We are not consciously aware of how our dedication to our devices might have limited our talk time and social opportunities in our embodied spaces.*

Source: *Deviced! Balancing Life and Technology in a Digital World* by Doreen Dodgen- Magee.

Her book is full of wisdom and practical things to try, with buckets of love and kindness. If you are struggling with any of this kind of stuff too, I highly recommend it as a healing tool to test you and support you.

This addiction to social media and screens is not the only out-of-balance or potentially toxic scenario on our planet at this time. If we took a proper look at things we would see so much that needs changing. The areas of our food industry which confuse us with chemicals, often with a view to get us 'hooked'. The pharmaceutical industry with millions 'hooked' on painkillers and opiates. The diet and beauty industry with their products full of chemicals, their marketing focused on shaming natural bodies and ageing in order to sell products. How badly we can treat the environment. How badly we treat each other. When you look into the 'tricks of the trade' there are multiple levels of manipulation and toxicity to see. Capitalist business. Patriarchy. Profit over people, over animals, over the earth.

This is part of a global human journey and the issues we currently face are not just a social media or Facebook issue. If we think of ourselves as one big organism, the holographic universe, the oneness, then where we are, and what I see, makes more sense to me.

Industries and corporations want us 'hooked' so they can make bigger profits, without considering or really truly caring about the effect it is having long-term on us humans, on our bodies, our mental health or our overall wellness and wellbeing.

There is a reason we have anxiety and health issues on the rise. Although we are waking up to this, I believe people-power and consumer actions will be what makes the most difference in the long run. Money talks.

We do have power. We *are* their product, their commodity, their consumers. We are the data. We are the users. We are the drug.

Governments and telecoms companies are soon going to be installing 5G in many parts of the western world, if they have not already started, without properly testing what it does to our physical bodies or to the environment long-term, to the bugs, the bees, the animals and the trees. From research I have seen, it is still unclear as to how these shortwave frequencies will affect all life over time, which is why places like Brussels and Japan (and Glastonbury!)

are saying no, not until more testing has been carried out.

As we move out of the Piscean Age and into the Aquarian Age, it is going to be up to each of us to play our part in cleaning up, healing up and growing up. Upgrading our timelines to the prophesied Golden Age.

> *The Aquarian Age will be dominated by networks, and information. The key to the astrological sign Aquarius is 'I know.' This is the age of information. Nothing is secret anymore. All information is available at your fingertips. Where the Piscean Age was organised in a vertical, up and down structure of hierarchies, the Aquarian Age is organised in a horizontal network, opening the world up to true equality.*

Source: 3ho: *The Aquarian Shift: What will be Different?* by Santokh Singh Khalsa, D.C.

With this happening at many levels of our society in lots of different ways, it may feel like some kind of planetary destiny. The old patriarchal energy has been at play in the shadow of industry and culture for as long as both the history books and I can remember. The birthing and return of the Mother, of feminine energy in 2020 is prepping to be powerful.

*In this next Wave sweeping the Event Horizon - the 2020-2030 Great Transformation - we are entering a time when transparency, authenticity and openness are going to be critical. This is not wishful New Age thinking but the only safe way to thrive. If you want to live peacefully, abundantly and congruently in the years to come, you must walk your talk. Why? Because your walk will be visible. If there is any degree of hypocrisy in your life, you are in danger of exposure. But think of it as having a wound cleaned or a bone reset when people expect you to operate in a way that is consistent with the values you express. So, wherever there is a dissonance between your value system and your actions, close the gap.*

Source: Lorna Bevan, *Hare In the Moon Astrology*. Monthly 5D Report for creatives, empaths, solopreneurs and outliers. (I have been to subscribed to this for years and love hareinthemoonastrology. co.uk)

Is this the apocalypse, the great unveiling, the great shift, the ascension, the wave which so many different civilisations, cultures and religious texts speak of? (As well as most of the spiritual community on my social media timeline and filter bubble.) If this is happening now, during this period we are now in, bringing everything into the light collectively, we might just change the trajectory to a betterment of ourselves and mankind.

The Holy Grail is us.

# INNER UNICORN QUESTION TIME

- *What are you looking for when you go online?*

- *Is it evolution for us to become merged with technology?*

- *Do you need a time out? Is there love? What needs to change?*

*Social media can be such an
amazing tool and it can be so
fun to share things but at the same
time it's a breeding ground for anxiety.
It's important to use social media in bite
sizes - as long as it makes me feel good,
and the second it doesn't,
I like to take some time away from it.
We should encourage kindness-
And be nicer to one another.
I feel like we'd all have a
much better experience
on social media if that was the case.*

Source: BBC News; Dua Lipa.

# #SOCIALMEDIAFORANEWAGE

# CHAPTER THREE:

# AUTHENTICITY, AUTHORITY & ACKNOWLEDGEMENT.

*'Be your authentic self' they say,*
*Amongst a sea of fake news we see every day.*
*The truth is in a state of decay.*
*With deep fakes and*
*propaganda making headway,*
*And when influencers steal words,*
*it is considered fair play.*
*Having it 'on good authority,'*
*Doesn't seem to take too much today.*
*Where 'fake it to make it'*
*seems to be 'the way.'*
*And buying Likes, follows and reviews -*
*mere childs-play.*
*So how to stay in your truth and not stray?*
*Even though it may not seem*
*to pay the same way,*
*I choose to be myself anyway.*
*Where karma maybe considered*
*by some a cliche,*
*It will only lead to your own judgement day.*

'Authenticity' has lost a lot of its meaning, or value, during recent years due to social media.

> *Authenticity has become something to be bought and sold. Dispatches of authentic self are posted into the empty vessels of social media so that they fill up, like a jar stuffed with Post-it notes about who we think, or hope, we are.*

Source: Pandora Sykes, from the pound project book, *The Authentic Lie.*

Being authentic *is* a good thing when it means being true to oneself and being genuine with others. For me, this is still one of the most important attributes of conscious communication.

> *Time to follow your authentic self even more. Dare to release fears deeper & to communicate, behave, show up as authentically You.*

Source: Facebook; by Sophie Grégoire.

There are many reasons we show up in different ways, with different people. The wanting to be liked. The protective ego. Thinking we have to do social media, to do life in a certain way to please others. Multiple, natural and nuanced versions of the self.

When our social media identities started to form, they needed the Likes, follows and shares to succeed, survive and thrive there. We adapted ourselves and created filtered and modified showreels, our branded profiles, editing what people see and what we share. It seems very natural to me. We change and filter memories in our minds depending on our perspective, so it is not a surprise that we edit forward with social media to create a picture we want to see of ourselves, or that we think others want to see. Or that marketing people think (or know) will sell. Not forgetting that it is fun having a creative profile, using all the new filters, stickers and gifs too. I LOVE a good GIF off! It is not all bad! But it can be confusing for us.

## What Does Authentic Feel Like for You?

I am going to share below some of the things we do on social media, in marketing or when creating, sharing and connecting with others online.

Take a few moments with each of these and use a little process that Ryan - *We Won't Die Wondering,* who runs an 'empowerment network' and coaching practice, where I co-facilitate workshops, shared with me;

> *I got really quiet this morning. I put one hand on my chest and one hand on my belly, and said to myself 'I am here, I am listening. What do you want me to know?'*

Feel into the following things and ask that Inner Unicorn of yours what it has to tell you...

- Buying reach through Facebook and Instagram ads.

- Using filters or professionally photographed /shopped images all the time.

- Posting on social media when you don't feel like posting.

- Employing a copywriter or social media manager to do it all for you.

- Buying influencer or media support without declaring it.

- Using NLP (if trained in it) in your content without declaring it.

- Using persuasive marketing tools to get people over the line or onto a list.

- Buying Likes or follows.

- Creating content inspired or created by others and not acknowledging them.

Some of those might feel a bit punchy to you. They are to me. Many have a middle ground, but it is good to consider how truly authentic these actions are for you and your business or how you could do them more consciously. I think that we could be more mindful of the tools and marketing advice available, and better assess what is now old paradigm and what is for a new age.

I am inviting you to question how it feels and not to just assume that because everyone else does it, or that it works to make money, that it is in alignment with you when using social media for your business.

Find your own Inner Unicorn answers, your own inner authority, your own inner compass to help guide you to the right course of action on social media and within your own marketing practices.

*By the power of the Grail,*
*which is hidden among dozens of false*
*grails; only the true Grail grants eternal*
*life, while a false one will kill the drinker.*

Source: Wikipedia, on
*Indiana Jones and The Last Crusade.*

# #SOCIALMEDIAFORANEWAGE

Motivational speaker and online influencer Jay Shetty has been called out for using other peoples words in his very popular and viral Facebook videos. Jay Shetty seems like a nice guy- I have friends who know him personally and say his energy is amazing- so what happened here?

YouTuber Nicole Arbour says of Jay Shetty:

> *Jay Shetty is just a professional meme reader. It's not like he reposted somebody else's meme, he crops their name out and puts in 'Jay Shetty'. That's stealing.*

Source: Doers Empire: IS JAY SHETTY ALSO A SCAM? YOUTUBER 'EXPOSES' MASSIVE CONTENT THEFT.

Did he make a mistake? Did his team? He hasn't apologised or spoken to the scandal publicly from what I can see. Despite the large amount of rather compelling evidence shared by Nicole, which was seen by millions, nothing bad seems to have happened or changed for Jay. He is still posting the same kind of content everyday and receiving tens of thousands of likes from his followers (I did unfollow him though).

I had a new client recently ask me if I thought it was ok to buy Likes. They knew of other spiritual teachers and practitioners doing this.

My response was that if spiritual teachers and leaders are buying Likes and follows, then we have definitely have an issue with how we feel about ourselves, our authenticity and authority online.

It really has nothing to do with the numbers, especially where numbers and words can be manipulated. The Wall Street Journal released a very interesting article looking at the influencer epidemic, *Online Influencers Tell You What to Buy, Advertisers Wonder Who's Listening.*

> '*A company, which didn't get its expected sales boost, sent an anonymous survey to their influencers, asking if they had ever paid for followers, likes or comments. Nearly two-thirds of respondents said yes,*' Mr. Ankarlid, the CEO, of A Good Company said.
>
> *HypeAuditor, an analytics firm, investigated 1.84 million Instagram accounts and found more than half used fraud to inflate the number of followers. Some influencers had large numbers of followers who weren't real people, meaning the accounts had been bought or were inactive, according to Anna Komok, HypeAuditor's marketing manager.*

Source: Wall Street Journal, '*Online Influencers Tell You What to Buy, Advertisers Wonder Who's Listening*' by Suzanne Kapner and Sharon Terlep.

Influencers are now required by law to mark posts with #ad or #promo, but I have noticed that this can still appear unclear. Watching Love Island (big reality TV show for those that don't know) where contestants often amass over a million followers whilst on the show, then cash in on their new found influencer status has been a good lesson in this, as some paid partnerships can be painful to watch whereas an endorsement that feels genuine is easy for me to spot.

Inspiring body-positive influencer Megan Jane Crabbe's promotion with The Body Shop is a great example. Megan (@bodyposipanda) is someone I respect as having great social media ethics and skills. I enjoy and recommend watching the way she handles social media and being an influencer.

It is not just the words we read or how many follower numbers we see that impacts our perceptions of authenticity and authority. I write about it like it is a new problem, but if we think about the mainstream media, how celebrities and models have been photoshopped, how we have been manipulated and spun by marketeers, journalists, advertisers, corporations and politicians our whole lives, then we should not really be surprised that social media works this way. The world works this way. Or it did.

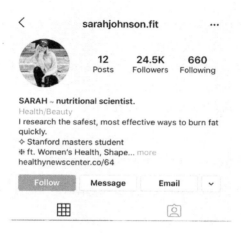

As I was working on this chapter, a post I saw alerted me to a whole new level of marketeers faking it on social media...

> *Ok wow, consider this my entrance into social media advocacy. I'm f\* fuming. Meet 'Sarah Johnson', a Stanford masters student who claims to have done extensive research on weight loss and has all of the safe, proven answers to keep you skinny forever. She's rampant on meme accounts and has tens of thousands of followers. AND SHE'S NOT EVEN REAL. The fine print on the link in 'her' bio even says so. Have we really stooped*

*THIS low as a society where we need to trick people into buying weight loss pills? Are we hurting for money THAT bad that we don't even care how we make it? I have NO clue how to go about getting this filth removed from instagram, but I'm hoping that someone who does can see this post and help me figure it out. I'm upset and you should be too. End rant.*

Source: Instagram, Natalie Windle @nataliewindle (with permission to share in full).

This is what the disclaimer on the website says:

*The story depicted on this site and the person depicted in the story are not real. Rather this story is based on the results that some people using these products have achieved…. The depictions on this page are fictitious and indicative of potential results. Actual results may vary.*

For a long time I have had the feeling that not all influencers and accounts are real, that it is possible to construct a character who exists online, but who does not exist offline. An account that is then selling digital or physical products and services through social media, pretending to be a real person. It is interesting to see some proof. In a world with AI Influencers, digital avatar supermodels and deep fakes in the market place, we need to be careful about what we see and believe online as 'authentic'.

*Technology can be used to make people believe something is real when it is not.*

Source: CNBC: Peter Singer, cybersecurity and defence focused strategist and senior fellow at New America.

But it isn't just the technology itself that can fool us- the problem also lies in how we use the technology to fool others. A recent scandal in the world of mummy-bloggers highlighted this when Clemmie Hooper, of @Mother_ of_Daughters fame, came out about a fake account she had created to fight to criticism, which ended up with her using it to troll others herself.

*I decided without telling anyone else that I would make an anonymous account so that this group of people would believe I was one of them, so that I could maybe change their opinions from the inside to defend my family and I. It became all-consuming and it grew bigger than I knew how to handle. When the users started to suspect it was me, I made the mistake of commenting about others. I regret it all and am deeply sorry - I know this has caused a lot of pain. Undoubtedly I got lost in this online world and the more I became engrossed in the negative commentary, the more the situation escalated. Engaging in this was a huge mistake, I take full responsibility for what's happened and I am just so sorry for the hurt I have caused to everyone involved including my friends and family.*

Source: Instagram Stories: Clemmie Hooper @ mother_of_daughters.

This highlights how detrimental social media can be personally and professionally if it gets out of control in this way. And with such tools so readily available to us, the use of discernment and our own inner authority is a priority.

*The importance of information in our society, presents the need for us to develop adequate skills to successfully navigate information. We need to consider not only the information we consume but also the information we produce – the information we share about ourselves – to gain a better understanding of this complex area and the impact it has on our personal beliefs, values, and society more broadly.*

Source: FutureLearn; Digital Wellbeing Course by the University of York.

Author: Susan Halfpenny.

# #SOCIALMEDIAFORANEWAGE

I am being asked more than ever for tips on how to show up authentically, how to BE ourselves on social media. I cover some of this in book one, ways to recognise if we are using it from our *social media soul vs our social media ego.* Rather than being a version of ourselves we think everyone wants to see and hear, rather than having several different identities online, and instead being our true, authentic selves across all platforms. Using it as a space where we are consistently being OURSELVES, trusting ourselves to *be* ourselves, wherever we go or inhabit, online or offline- remembering that the consistent part is YOU.

It feels like such a simple thing, yet the way we are viewed by others is also very much dependent on their perception of us, rather than just our perception of ourselves. We live in a world of perceptions and projections with social media like a FunFair House of Mirrors in the cloud; who knows what we might see when we catch a glimpse of our reflection.

*Bottom line- 2020's epochal astrology is all about power. There is enormous potential to amplify your own beyond anything you've experienced before but you have to refuse to be hypnotised into witnessing the 3D world burn by mirroring and modelling the highest expression of Pluto-impeccable Truth and Radical Honesty.*

Source: Lorna Byrne, *Hare In the Moon Astrology,* 5D report.

# Cloud of Co-creation

It isn't just the likes of Jay Shetty who use other people's words and ideas without acknowledging them properly. Life is a co-creation. We are not always conscious of it in a space where we pick up so much from each other through books, videos, messenger chats, emails, texts and posts. We are one big cloud of co-creation and ideas can jump between people, as Elizabeth Gilbert describes in her book *Big Magic*.

We pay for content, trainings and coaching; we read other people's books and we pick up ideas from all of those interactions, which become weaved into our own offerings. It is surely a natural, normal thing in this day and age with so much information being absorbed at warp speed by our brains like never before.

But if we do know, and we are trying to be more mindful of what our sources are, there are a great many ways to acknowledge others.

Social media is a great place to start.

*Whenever I sound like I know what I'm talking about regarding astrology it's because I follow @theleokingdom. He brings it to a whole new level. Thank you Leo King for sharing your wisdom.*

Source: Instagram: @healwithalana.

Acknowledgement could be inviting someone to speak on your podcast or Facebook Live, to collaborate as a guest teacher at a workshop or online event. It could come through shouting them out in an Instagram story or post. It could come from sharing an honest story about who has inspired you. It could come in the form of leaving a review and posting it so everyone can see. It could be sending an Amazon voucher, or a little gift if someone speaks on your podcast or video call, like my friend Lucy Anne Chard did for me after she interviewed me as part of a coaching course.

It was lovely to receive and I felt very acknowledged by her gesture.

In a world that moves so fast, when we are quickly moving on to the next email, the next post, the next WhatsApp message, the next person, it can be easy to take each others time, energy and contribution for granted. There is kindness and generosity of spirit in making an effort to acknowledge others and this is something I would like to do more of myself and see more of in *Social Media For A New Age - The Next Phase: 2020 and Beyond.* As we become more aware of it, we need to take responsibility for acknowledging others.

It is not just acknowledging each other but also acknowledging our lineages that is such an important part of this, which Henrietta, my friend and founder of Sacred Leadership brought to my attention recently. In a world where cultural appropriation is not always properly considered, thinking of how we pay respect and appreciation when it is due is important in moving towards a fair and equal future. Cultural appropriation vs cultural appreciation is a big topic for debate online, an area which creates a lot of tension, sometimes quite rightly so. At other times, however, it is fuelled by the call-out culture on social media.

*Acknowledgement is far reaching across all nations, cultures and land masses. It can be as simple as recognising someone as a photographer of an image you choose to use, a piece of wisdom that has been passed down to you from an Elder, or a skill you have been taught.*

*Ultimately, it comes down to respect and gratitude, for what we co-create together.*

*And honouring the origins of how it came into being. Nothing is done alone. There is always a bigger story. And it's time for that bigger story, and the people behind it, to be seen. Especially our indigenous peoples, and our women. The dream walkers and the life givers. Who create and birth the new into the world.*

Source: Facebook; Henrietta Gothe Ellis, *Sacred Leadership, A new Template for Humanity. The alchemy of love, power and wisdom.*

# INNER UNICORN QUESTION TIME

- *How do you know what you are seeing online is real, true or authentic?*

- *Do you trust metrics as a mark of authority?*

- *How do you acknowledge others and their intellectual property?*

*This is a time to set our intentions for empowering our lives - transforming ourselves into our spiritual quest. Whether you want to call that Camelot or a Grail quest, that's how I like to look at it, I feel that the story is replaying right now, and the whole understanding of it, however you want to look at it...*
*The Holy Grail, that Holy Grail energy is the purity of your soul, and the higher mission that it is here to do.*
*This is not a time for us to just f\*ck around.*
*This is where the test is.*

Source: YouTube; HighVibe TV; David Palmer, The Leo King, Deep Astrology Weekly Horoscope all signs Nov 5-11 2019 Jupiter shadow, Saturn Neptune Completion.

**#SOCIALMEDIAFORANEWAGE**

# PART TWO:

# THE NEXT PHASE: 2020 AND BEYOND

# CHAPTER FOUR:

# PREDICTIONS & FUTURE PROOFING

*Change is a constant, of that we can be sure,*
*The digital revolution wants*
*us online more and more.*
*With data more valuable*
*than gold these days,*
*Neural interfaces are on the way...*
*Facebook's no longer just a*
*digital town square,*
*Mark's moved into our living room,*
*Bringing us a new Horizon on his way there.*
*Augmented and virtual realities,*
*Instead of walking outside amongst the trees.*
*If we can look up from our mobile*
*for long enough to see,*
*We can create a world where*
*we take responsibility.*
*Viewing our technology more mindfully,*
*Stopping before we connect*
*everything we own to 5G.*
*Securing new rights to our data privacy,*
*And freeing ourselves from*
*this digital primacy.*

# Moving from the 'Town Square to the Living Room'.

In a post titled *A Privacy Focused Vision for Social Networking*, Zuckerberg shares:

> *Over the last 15 years, Facebook and Instagram have helped people connect with friends, communities, and interests in the digital equivalent of a town square. But people increasingly also want to connect privately in the digital equivalent of the living room. As I think about the future of the internet, I believe a privacy-focused communications platform will become even more important than today's open platforms.*

Source: Facebook, Mark Zuckerberg.

His vision is about communication, *privacy-focused* communication. The move from the *Town Square to the Living Room* is an important one to take note of when thinking about the future of social media, marketing, promotion and our communication. Everything we do on social media is a communication. A transmission. A signal. A sign. To one another or to ourselves.

The dynamic balance between these spaces - the where, how and how often we communicate in digital spaces- is changing, especially if and when we don't want to be on social media so much. There isn't a formula for this. Finding a personal way to create, use and flow with the platforms and digital spaces gives us insight, power and sovereignty.

In thinking about the *Town Hall to the Living Room,* and reflecting that to think about where we work best, we gain an understanding of the difference nuances of each of those spaces. How many people, profiles and identities do we have? By thinking of these as real places where we exist, we begin to get more intentional with the time we spend there. We have the opportunity to create different kinds of *Living Rooms*, perhaps re-naming them *Digital Workshop Spaces*, *Studios*, or *Consultancy Rooms*, or as my friends Nicola and Maja have done, a *Temple Space*. But instead of doing it all on Facebook, I want to look at ways of doing this elsewhere, without needing the upfront investment of website or app development.

I want to share an excerpt from a Zoom chat I had with Benji Vaughan, the founder of Disciple Media, a community app with clients including Peta Jean, the author of *Earth is Hiring*. His team have built an interesting product with the aim to help people build authentic online communities, away from Facebook, with a variety of different ways to communicate, as well as to monetise.

Katie: *My thoughts around Social Media For A New Age is that we trusted Facebook with the town square, and I'm not necessarily willing to trust them with my living room.*

Benji: *No, I wouldn't trust them, I wouldn't let them through the front door. It's interesting, I think that it's funny that he uses that analogy, because we've often used that analogy; saying that Facebook is the town square and we're the conversations in the pubs and cafes. We try and not become Facebook bashers, whatever my personal opinions might be. I simply think it's a bad product for communities.*

*The hypothesis we have is that Facebook, because it was in the first wave of social media platforms, it ended up trying to do everything. Because it was a new market, so they were like, 'Okay, we're going to have messaging and news and feeds and connections and groups, and it's going to do absolutely everything on one platform.' And as social experiences amongst systems has become a ginormous trend, having it all within one platform has become unwieldy and dangerous, and actually, the messages coming from Facebook at the moment are that it wants to double down on messaging.*

*The way the future looks in my eyes is that as a citizen you only ever interact with two types of body, you interact with people and you interact with institutions, and by Institution I mean in the broadest sense you see; a cohort of people brought together round a certain interest, whether that's a brand or a type of yoga. Messaging is extremely good for the one to one or one to a small group of friends. We're trying to build a really effective way for you to communicate and interact with a body of people, i.e. a community or an institution.*

*Community is much more than belonging to something; it's about doing something together that makes belonging matter.*

Source: Instagram @briansolis Brian Solis, digital analyst and anthropologist, futurist and author of *Life Scale*.

# #SOCIALMEDIAFORANEWAGE

# Will We Leave Facebook?

*Just look at what happened to MySpace...*

Facebook have much bigger digital properties and with that much more power than MySpace or any other competitors have ever had. I noticed some of the congressmen practically salivating at Mark's power when he was testifying at Capitol Hill. But never say never. Who knows what this next decade is going to bring.

> *Pluto was transiting through Capricorn during the birth of the U.S - the sign that rules the patriarchy, government and capitalism— all of which are already in an advanced process of collapse. Be ready for a karmic shift in the levers of power as the polarisation of views and tribes intensifies, secession becomes more than an idea and America's role in the world undergoes a radical change.*

Source: Lorna Bevan, *Hare In The Moon Astrology, 5D report* - for creatives, empaths, solopreneurs and outliers.

I have been re-thinking how much I promote, naturally through my work, the use of Facebook's social media platforms. Finding better ways to use it as a communication tool and not an attention trap. Evaluating how much we have come to rely on it. It does concern me to be too reliant on the good graces of Facebook Inc, or rather, FACEBOOK.

This is something my email marketeer friends warned me about years ago. Email isn't social media. It is different. As a channel, I feel it has also been sullied by marketeers, which I discuss in my first book. And even though the mighty Facebook may not be going anywhere anytime soon, our relationship to it is shifting. The energy of the platform is changing.

Being conscious and aware of this shift is worth thinking about when future-proofing. If more people deactivate their accounts or simply create better habits, spending less time and reliance on Facebook, we will naturally see the reach of content and connection reduce there.

If we really do start to see device time and social media as a social stigma, like many people see smoking now, this will impact Facebook. Consumer power is our biggest strength, which I don't see as a bad thing.

*Salesforce CEO Marc Benioff, who one year ago bought Time magazine for $150 million,* *blasted Facebook this week calling it 'the new cigarette.' He tweeted, 'FB is the new cigarette – it's addictive, bad for us, & our kids are being drawn in.'*

Source: New York Post; *Time owner slams Facebook as 'the new cigarette',* by Kieth J Kelly.

New platforms will emerge. Or Facebook will change.

Different ways of using social media positively will come to the light.

*The Campfire Convention*, as I mentioned earlier, is somewhere to consider if you want to create, share and converse with people about social issues and cultural commentary. Maybe membership sites and community sites are the new social media. Making some space to do it in a different way and ditching the mindless scrolling to become a better digital citizen is a way I want to try to play.

For younger generations new platforms such as TikTok seem to be capturing their time and attention. MeWe is another social media platform I have heard people mention, but I do not see either of those currently working in the social media culture and community that I or my clients are a part of. I don't think that we, or I, will stop using Facebook's tools any time soon, unless something really big happens. The sheer size of the network, how many people we can connect and communicate with there is phenomenal; we should be looking to future-proof, adopting a different strategy for content distribution and looking for ways to connect outside of Facebook.

As my relationship to social media shifts and as I manage to get a better balance of my intentional technology and social media usage, will the way I produce, consume and post content change?

I think the answer to that has to be yes.

# How Do You Like Me Now?

*We've become reliant on numbers, so we let them stand in for meaning more than they do. Remove the integers and we might find our digital Shangri-la. Or at least a slightly healthier, more sustainable life online.*

Source: Wired; Quote by Benjamin Grosser (creates ' demetricators' for social media); *My Life online without all the metrics,* by Arielle Pards.

Likes and follows created a gamification culture on social media, turning it into a popularity contest in the cloud, creating low levels of anxiety for many people taking part. Everyone that I work with obviously wants to build or grow their presence on the platforms, which means increasing either Likes on a page or Likes on a post.

I see first-hand how much this aspect of the gamification can impact our wellbeing. *The social media vortex of doom* is the phrase I use to describe when we start basing our value and the value of the work we are doing in the world on how many followers we have, gain or lose.

I don't know if you have ever done this yourself, but let's say you have written something that feels vulnerable or a post that you have worked really hard on and you think is really good; but, you post it and nothing happens. Social media crickets and tumbleweeds blow through your notifications and it feels like the worst thing that could happen. No Likes, no comments, nothing. So you question yourself, consider deleting the post, or you do actually delete it. Of course the opposite can also happen where you share a picture of your dog, or a silly in-the-moment post, which then gets hundreds of Likes.

A lot of this is down to humans, but a lot is also down to the algorithms. If you don't know how the Facebook algorithms work, basically the more people that like a post, the more people get to see a post. More post Likes = higher post reach. And no Likes = no or very little reach.

I still have to remind myself not to get sucked into the Likes dynamic of being on social media, but it is hard. I see that how much engagement and how much reach we get can impact our self-esteem.

It is the metric we have been given and taught equals success. Instagram feels like it has become the game of 'Influencer' and the prize is advertising dollars or sales, which make people play the social media game even more.

It is also the main dopamine delivery method, those pesky Likes that have me picking up my phone to check to see how many a post has, and I personally feel that it drives a lot of my social media addiction.

As the meaning of 'Likes' has evolved in our digital society, I began to see it like a virus, creating comparison, anxiety and judgement as individuals, internally, externally and amongst us collectively.

The Like landscape is in fact changing. Instagram are currently testing hiding Likes in seven countries including Australia, New Zealand and most recently in the USA. Adam Mosseri, Instagram CEO said of hiding Likes at the Wired 25 conference:

> *The idea is to try and depressurise Instagram, make it less of a competition, give people more space to focus on connecting with the people that they love, things that inspire them. But it's really focused about young people on young people. We have to see how it affects how people feel about their platform, how it affects how they use the platform, how it affects the creator ecosystem. But I've been spending a lot of time on this personally.*

To clarify, Instagram will be hiding your Likes from other users, but you will still be able to see your own Likes. It will be interesting to see how this impacts the platform. I wonder if people will stop liking posts because they can't see their Likes showing up; if that's the case then the algorithm won't work in the same way anymore, as reach will be reduced, and we could end up feeling worse because we see post Likes drop.

> It's still too early to gauge whether social media demetrication improves a user's mental health or the quality of online discourse. If it does work, it could be an important step to bringing users back to platforms that they have been using less frequently or abandoning.

Source: Wired; *Instagram Will Test Hiding 'Likes' in the US Starting Next Week*

*Hiding like counts is just the latest step in Instagram's quest to become the safest place on the internet.*

> *Removing 'Likes' won't remove comparison culture.*

Source: Instagram: Jocelyn at Cyber psychologist @ digital_nutrition.

*I am super aware of how 'likes' influence how I both create and consume.*

Source: Instagram; Anna Sansom; @ anna_sansom_writer.

Even Jack Doresy, Twitter CEO admitted this recently on his TED Talk 'How Twitter Needs to Change', saying:

*If I had to start the service again, I would not emphasise the 'like' count as much, I don't think I would even create 'like' in the first place.*

Source: Twitter; Jack Dorsey @JackDorsey.

We can lurk behind Likes, thinking we are entering a conversation. I hold my hands up in doing this: it's quick, it's easy, it is a nod of appreciation, and those Likes do feel good, dammit. Likes can be a sweet thing when done with intention; they can be sign of appreciation, acknowledgement, an energy exchange. Likes aren't all bad.

*Whoever you enjoy following on here, whatever accounts light you up, let them and the algorithms know by 'liking' their stuff. It's actually a really powerful way to support someone's work and business \*and\* make* *sure you to see more of their free content. It's also a powerful energy exchange! An inspiring or useful post for a quick tap? Sounds like a good deal to me!*

Source: Instagram; Vix New Age Hipster @ newagehipster333.

*Count your blessings not your followers.*
*The only like that matters is your own.*
*Your worth is not*
*determined by numbers.*
*Happiness is not an algorithm.*

Source: Instagram: @Timetologoff.

## Switching It Up

When Lush, a big natural cosmetics brand announced they were closing their Instagram account, marketing experts said they were crazy. Yet what I noticed was that Lush aren't leaving social media altogether, they simply said that they are 'switching it up'.

> *We're switching up social. Increasingly, social media is making it harder and harder for us to talk to each other directly. We are tired of fighting with algorithms, and we do not want to pay to appear in your newsfeed. So we've decided it's time to bid farewell to some of our social channels and open up the conversation between you and us instead.*

Source: Instagram: @LushUK.

Doing something different doesn't mean quitting social all together. I think it is great to keep asking questions about what is or is not working for you.

> *We want social to be more about passion and less about likes.*

> *This isn't the end. It's just the start of something new.*

Source: Instagram; Lush UK @lushuk.

Lush clearly believe in their brand enough to be confident that their customers will go where they need to.

> We believe we can make more noise using all of our voices across the globe because when we do, we drive change, challenge norms and create a cosmetic revolution.

Source: Instagram; Lush UK @lushuk.

They are challenging the current pay-to-play Facebook landscape in order to focus on community. I find it inspiring and I look forward to seeing their revolution in action.

Reading the thousands of comments on Lush's Instagram, people seem to love it:

> "Fabulously refreshing…" "I appreciate it so much, congrats!"

> " Lush leading the way as always". "This warms my heart"

> "Great initiative, let's become humans again." "Be revolutionary!"

> "I think absolutely everyone should follow suit– this is such an amazing idea."

Although a few people did comment to say…

*"Marketing suicide."*

*"A huge step backwards.' "I'm rlly disappointed."*

Source: @LushUK on Instagram, *.We're switching things up.*

I am going to reach out to Lush UK to see if I can speak to someone there about what kind of difference switching it up has made and how their customers and employees feel since they left Instagram. Lush are a forward-thinking, 'human' company who even put their employees faces on their products. If they agree, I will share my findings at a later date online, somewhere.

Just remember that we can't please everyone.

There will always be someone who doesn't agree.

Thats OK. You gotta do you.

# Polarised People, Polarised Planet.

How opinionated are we feeling these days? Ummmmm... let me just look in a few comment threads for a moment, shall I? It can be testy, tetchy, bitchy at times, depending on what you post and how much your posts polarise people.

I have not been subjected to trolling personally, but I have friends who have. It can cause all kinds of anxiety. Thankfully it is getting more coverage and attention than it has before because cyberbullying is a serious issue.

We can behave very differently when there is a screen between us and someone else. From texts, to posts, to comments, we can be very reactive through digital means. We can also be very misunderstood, and be very affected by what we receive online.

We have developed an outpouring of outrage and a digital culture of calling people out.

Obama spoke to this at his Foundation's latest summit:

> *Mr Obama said that calling people out on social media did not bring about change, and that change was complex.*

*'This idea of purity and you're never compromised and you're politically woke, and all that stuff -- you should get over that quickly. The world is messy. There are ambiguities. People who do really good stuff have flaws.'*

Source: BBC News: *Barack Obama challenges 'woke' culture.*

People are scared and angry. Social media is in the middle of all of this, and it may get worse before it gets better. It often takes us to become outraged, to see the sickness and feel the things in order to take action.

*I want to be around people that do things. I don't want to be around people anymore that judge or talk about what people do. I want to be around people that dream and support and do things.*

Source: Instagram @somethingdani : Quote by Amy Poehler, actress.

I want to see us using social media to communicate our presence, our essence and our action in this world, as a way to lead by example and as a tool to keep ourselves accountable as well.

Peta Jean, author of *Earth is Hiring*, who I appreciate as a voice on social media to speak her truth, says:

> *Only now after years of high horsery when it came to what I cared about, I do my personal activism a little differently. Activism is beautiful. I love seeing the many roars being roared. The biggest thing on earth I am anti is missing the point. I have seen super spiritual 'heart centred' people be ruder and nastier than anyone I've ever known. I've seen vegan activists preach compassion yet show zero for a single mum buying meat for her kids with money she'd saved for weeks. I've seen a lot of missing the point, righteousness and high horsery including in MYSELF.*

Source: Instagram, Peta Jean @petajean Peta Kelly, Nobody's coach. Author of *Earth Is Hiring* and *Earth to Kids*.

Social media is full of activists with big opinions. Trolls with broken hearts. Grumpy, angry reviewers. We need to start thinking more about how a negative post, comment or text may affect the person receiving it on the other side, as we express our opinion.

*What Do YOU think
about call-out culture?
If the price of entry to the public
debate is personal perfection, then
we're f\*'d. But if the price is simply a
shared aspiration to improve the world,
to create a better collective, to create
ideals for us to move towards knowing
that we can immediately realise them
by being forgiving towards one another
when we inevitably slip, by encouraging
these new virtues and new ideals, surely
that's what we should be doing. Instead
of condemning individuals, making
individuals culpable for social,
and cultural problems.
We need new systems, new ideals.*

Source: Instagram, Russell Brand @russellbrand,

*What Do YOU think about call-out culture?*

# #SOCIALMEDIAFORANEWAGE

Dr Phil Parker, creator of the Lightening Process which focuses on the science behind how the brain and body interact, kindly applied his wisdom and knowledge to one of my Inner Unicorn Questions, which you can watch on my IGTV channel.

He shares:

> *The comments that we see or give out affect people in an unbalanced way. In a ratio of 4:1 - negative comments will affect us more powerfully than positives. So we need to make sure we are actively seeking out and giving out the positive.*

Source: Instagram, Dr Phil Parker @thephilparker.

Social media can literally polarise our brains 4:1- negative to positive - and this could be happening to you every time you tap into social media, which could be more than 85 times a day, for hours EVERY SINGLE DAY. This is doing things to our brain chemistry on a daily basis and not all of it is good for us.

As I mentioned earlier, Dr Doreen Dodgen-Magee's book *Deviced!* is the best thing I have read on this subject, and it has helped me with tools to manage day-to-day and to recognise more about the impact my digital use has on my life. Today I listened to her speak on a podcast for the first time and soft tears ran down my face as I listened to the different ways tech is affecting us, and as I recognised some of my own issues. If you like my work, I think that you would enjoy and benefit from what she has to share. Her words, both written and spoken, have been received by my nervous system as a sweet healing dose.

We do have the power to change things through our thoughts and actions. When we change ourselves, we change the world. If we want heaven on earth, if we want the new earth and the new age, we balance these polarisations.

I often talk about digital vs physical, the digital dimension, about how we get into alignment between our physical and digital selves and how we traverse the digital dimension energetically with our digital avatar. Looking more carefully at our identities in cyberspace, how are they congruent and consistent with our whole self? How are we behaving when we are in digital land, outside of our physical selves, but still ultimately part of our whole self? Doreen frames this thinking in a much tidier way in *Deviced!*. She writes:

*The reality is that our digital and embodied lives come together to create one real, whole life - a real life that includes both.*

Source: *Deviced!* by Doreen Dodgen-Magee.

I have spent a lot of time in the digital ethers this past decade or more, and it's taken me having a break to come back inside myself a little more, to see how I, like so many, am disconnecting from my embodied life because of technology. I know now that I need to find and create a much better balance.

This is a recognition, this is a remembrance, this is coming home to ourselves. Integrating these pieces, the digital self with the embodied self, as Doreen so perfectly describes it. Merging the selves, so we are operating as one throughout the dimensions, digital or otherwise.

# Virtual and Augmented Reality in a New Age

*Avatars: Are we ready for our digital twins? When most of us think of avatars, we imagine a tall, blue movie character. Today they are being used in a very different way. Our digital doubles could soon be working for us, or maybe even replacing us, according to the US tech industry.*

Source: *'My Avatar & Me'* by Amelia Hemphill, Sebastien Rabas, Katie Arnold and Owen Kean for BBC 100 Women on BBC iPlayer.

Did you know that brands are already using digital avatar models in their marketing and that actual AI Avatar Instagram influencers exist?

Since 2016, when the first AI Instagram influencer Lil Miquela appeared on the social media scene, digital models have been in the market place. The fashion industry in particular has embraced CGI models, using them in campaigns for the likes of Prada and Louis Vuitton.

Cameron James Wilson, the creator of digital model Shudu (@shudu.gram) shares the ethical debate he had with himself over this:

*'I had a lot of internal debate, philosophically and ethically,' he recalls. 'A lot of people thought she was real, and I felt uncomfortable about this. Now, I try to make it apparent that it's me behind the account. Being honest and transparent means that I can open people's eyes to the programmes that are out there and what they can do. The problem with images is that we're hardwired into believing that they're real.'*

Source: Vogue UK: *The Numerous Questions Around The Rise Of CGI Models And Influencers,* by Alice Newbold.

But we can't trust that all creators will do the same. Much like the fake account created on Instagram selling slimming pills that I shared earlier, it may not be clear: the truth may be hidden in the small print as to whether something is real or not. Where does the moral dilemma lie when we are talking about businesses using virtual reality, augmented reality and artificial intelligence? There is nowhere easier to do this than on social media.

*'I, myself, am looking to generate cash flow through designing models for brands who want a digital spokesperson,' Wilson shares. 'As we move into the VR space, it's inevitable*

*that companies will want to communicate to potential customers on these platforms.'*

Source: Vogue UK: *The Numerous Questions Around The Rise Of CGI Models And Influencers,* by Alice Newbold.

With reportedly more than $3 billion dollars invested into virtual reality, Facebook announced its Social VR world and platform 'Horizon' alongside new 'immersive' technology, investing another $1 billion into neural interfaces by acquiring CTRL-labs.

*According to a new Forbes report:*

> *More than 100 MILLION consumers will use AR & VR to shop online and in-store by 2020.*

> *46% of businesses expect VR to become mainstream within the next 3 years.*

> *VR is expected to account for 40% of all B2B experiences by 2022. (????)*

> *Globally, VR software alone is predicted to be worth $6.4bn by 2022.*

Source: Linked In: Steven Bartlett CEO & founder at Social Chain.

When Mark Zuckerberg described Facebook's new immersive technology, with its neural interfaces at the Oculus Connect Developer Conference, it made me stop and think about this a little more deeply. And it made me consider if there are any alternative agendas, aside from the money.

> *Our technology vision is putting people at the centre of the computing experience. We do this by building technology that advances the feeling of presence. It is more immersive. We are getting the hardware out of the way. Creating better, more natural UI (user interfaces) and better, more realistic avatars.*

Source: Mark Zuckerberg's Keynote speech at the *Oculus Connect developer conference 2019.*

Is it possible for us to get lost in a virtual-reality world? To become less embodied and living our lives out in the digital dimension? I wonder what spending any amount of time as a digital avatar in this way might do to my wellbeing and mental health.

In Facebook's Horizon we will apparently be cartoon avatars of ourselves. I love the idea of being a cartoon avatar but I am concerned I may get lost in there, even if it would be cool to have a cup of tea in a virtual cafe with my friend Erin over in the USA. But if using filters to extend our eyelashes, covering up our wrinkles, widening our eyes, whitening our teeth or adding bunny ears is alluring, and I can be quite partial to some digital enhancement and the desire for eternal youth, then imagine what may happen if we spend more time as our VR avatars rather than as our embodied selves? That is pretty worrying to me and if those stats are anything to go by they seem to think that we might. The thought of everyone hooking up to the internet through a VR visor instead of through handheld device is like looking towards a dystopian future, as explored in the BBC documentary *Digital Twins* or the TV series *Black Mirror*.

However, the future is still unwritten and it may not become what Mark Zuckerberg and his mates hope for. Maybe, similar to Google Glasses, Horizon won't take off. It is up to us to decide and take action by how we adopt the technology.

Update: It has just been reported that Zuckerberg has spoken about the challenges Facebook face with the VR market during the company's Q3 earnings announcement; it appears there is a lack of interest by the general public.

*'On VR and AR, you're right. This is taking a bit longer than we thought. And I'm still optimistic,' Zuckerberg said. 'I think that the long-term vision and the reasons why I thought this — we're going to be important and big — are unchanged.'*

Source: Business Insider, *Mark Zuckerberg admits that Facebook's $2 billion bet on virtual reality 'is taking a bit longer than we thought' to pay off,* by Aaron Holmes.

# Digital Wellbeing

Digital wellbeing is turning into a big topic and because of that we need to be careful about not getting caught up in the hype. I am a little concerned about this creating a layer of lip service rather then meaningful action coming from big tech and big media.

> *Google's Paper Phone is the latest in a string of offerings attempting to grab the attention of an audience weary of the ever-expanding presence of tech in our lives, as well as the feeling of being chained to your phone. The Paper Phone is part of a new package of 'digital well-being experiments' that the company says is aimed at giving users a 'digital detox.' It arrived the same week Google launched its latest phone: the $800 Pixel 4, which has built-in radar technology that can be controlled by a user's hand motions.*

Source: The Washington Post; *Google's newest phone is literally just a piece of paper,"* by Marie C. Baca.

Digital tools for monitoring screen time have become more widely available across Facebook, Google, Microsoft and Apple products this past year. These tools range from being able to track your screen time to setting your phone to 'unavailable' or creating an alert to tell you to how long you have spent on an app that day. I have Instagram set to alert me at 1 hour 10 minutes and I will try to reduce that time. It does help. It is really showing me how fast an hour can pass; I got an alert saying 1 hour 10 minutes had passed before I had breakfast the other day. It would be really helpful if there was a snooze button which would then tell me if I have spent another 10 minutes or more past the curfew. I can often ignore it, because I'm using it for it for work and then get lost in a scroll by accident.

*Although there is currently no proof that these wellbeing tools will change behaviours, understanding our habits and reflecting on them can be the first step to making positive changes in our relationship with technology.*

Source: FutureLearn; Digital Wellbeing Course by the University of York.

In my own recognition of needing help with my digital wellbeing and mindfulness, I see how important it also is for the lives of my clients, my friends, for you and ultimately for the future of mankind.

The Royal Society for Public Health have a new e-learning resource called *Looking after your Self-ie - A guide to finding your balance on and offline,* which may be a good place to start- and it's free.

I am on my own journey of developing a better relationship to technology. I am still working out the best ways to integrate this into who I am, how I work and what I offer in terms of supporting others and their work on social media. It is a massive game changer for me.

One thing I have not yet shared is the impact on my physical body the past twenty years of laptop and mobile device use has had. I have been managing a chronic pain issue for the past five years in my jaw, mouth and tongue. With diagnoses ranging from bruxism (teeth grinding) to TMJ and anxiety, no-one has really been able to diagnose it. Imagine what a really bad migraine might be like, but instead of it in my head, it is in my mouth. My tongue will buzz and feel like it is being pinched or squeezed. I can have a bad or good day, week or month. This year during a particularly bad flare up, I saw a lot of acupuncturists, cranial sacral practitioners, chiropractors and healers as well as the doctor. The conclusion is 'text neck' caused by bad posture when working at a laptop or mobile device.

Feeling the negative physical effects of my social media use in my body, as well as the impact it is having on my emotional and mental health, has been an almighty big wake-up call to improve my wellbeing and to understand the role my relationship with technology plays in that.

# INNER UNICORN QUESTION TIME

- *What platforms feel best for you to explore, for your highest good and for your wellbeing, when using social media to connect and communicate with others?*

- *If Social VR becomes mainstream over the next few years, will you use it to connect with your friends, clients and customers instead of through a mobile device? Can you see this happening in your home or workplace?*

- *How could you switch up your social media habits to be more in alignment with YOUR social media ethics and in a way that supports your wellbeing?*

*Technology is cool, but you've got to use it as opposed to letting it use you.*

Prince

Source: Today Show; *His Purple Highness;*

*'Today' host Matt Lauer talks to 'The Artist.'*

# #SOCIALMEDIAFORANEWAGE

# PART THREE:

# DIGITAL SELF-CARE

# CHAPTER FIVE:

# LOVE, LIGHT AAAND ACTION

*As I struggle to be at peace with Facebook,*
*Because I cannot shake the feeling*
*that Zuck is a crook.*

*It's been more difficult for me to*
*see the positive side,*

*I forget how amazing it is we can*
*communicate world wide.*

*The internet, our cyber space,*

*Where we can connect heart to heart,*
*with love and grace.*

*It is up to us to be the change we*
*want to see on this planet,*

*One by one, together, letting the*
*unfoldment be organic.*

*Using technology to support us naturally,*

*Not letting it become a global tragedy.*

*We need to invest in our digital wellbeing,*

*Reduce distractions, the addictions and all*
*the bad that we're seeing.*

*Booming the web up with our*
*loving energetic light,*

*using it consciously, a place*
*where we treat each other right.*

*Creating Social Media For A New Age,*

*Where we are not prisoners of*
*Facebook's gilded cage,*

*Instead we are the*
*leaders, sacred and true,*

*With social media a tool, that*
*connects me and you.*

*This is a deep healing phase. The crazy we are seeing in the outside world is a sickness detox. We are coming to terms with seeing the sickness in our world right now and the sickness in us as humanity. And we can look at that in the outside world, but the best place for us to look is at ourselves as well. So be sure especially if you are a leader, a healer, a way shower, a teacher, it's a really important time to be able to bring ourselves back to centre and be able to balance.*

Source: YouTube; Lee Harris - *Monthly Energy Update* (November 2019).

This book has been quite a heavy process at times. So I am going to use this last chapter to make a commitment to change, to improving our social media experience with each baby step and giant leap at a time. Lightening the load, to create more flow to the framework than ever before, in order to enjoy new possibilities within our social media practice.

There is power and privilege in a space where we can communicate with each other worldwide; to be able to utilise the benefits it holds for us and not have it overwhelm us or drain us.

There is power in realising that measuring success by numbers and statistics does not show the whole picture, the richness or the depth of the interactions and experiences.

There is power in building a bridge to a more collective, collaborative, creative and conscious social media culture.

This is the new age that I dream of.

If we expand the viewpoint of social media away from all the sales messages, selfies and self-promotion and come up with some guidelines between us on how to use it for social good, for the good of ourselves and our society, we could change it completely.

We could begin seeing it as a connective space, 'a connective tissue between souls' as Karen Ruimy shared in my first book. We could begin flipping our perspective of what the internet is, what this worldwide informational highway is, by being more aware of the digital cloud that is all around us and how we co-create it.

It is a cloud with a silver lining. There is community here.

I remember this each time I connect with someone properly- a friend, client, or colleague- through digital means, when I am present to them and their words, their digital avatar in all its forms. As I receive them, I take a moment to feel their words and hear them through the digital dimension.

Being able to be energetically in two (if not more) places at the same time can be such a gift. One of my besties, Henrietta, is in Australia and often on the move. Technology keeps us in communication and keeps us connected in a really beautiful way. I know how social media connects the soul family every day, the beautiful loving energy that can reach us wherever we are across the world. The fact that many of us have found true connections and friendships online is a testament to the beneficial power of social media.

We feel each other through the messages, posts, emails and DMs we send. They are our digital soul songs that transmit our tones and our frequencies.

*I keep coming back to this.*
*Targeted and specific usage.*
*To boom the light out*
*through the internet…*
*Screen time becomes #upgradetime,*
*then we migrate from screen to*
*in-person gatherings. Organically.*
*To #superupgrades in the physical.*

Source: Henrietta Gothe Ellis, *Sacred Leadership,*
*A new Template for Humanity.*
*The alchemy of love, power and wisdom.*

# #SOCIALMEDIAFORANEWAGE

# Upgrading our Digital Identity

Creating a personalised approach for our platforms is paramount for us in this new age of social media, as we all have different needs, uses, skills, enjoyment and relationships within the digital domain. I want to use this final section to help upgrade our digital identity and wellbeing. It would be great if you could try some of these with me and let me know how you get on, ok?

If you have got this far with the book, and enjoy what I have shared, I consider you a part of a #socialmediaforanewage comm-unity.

Comm-unity.

Communication that unites us.

If you are reading this you are likely to be using social media for work and play; we are united in this activity. We have connected through the words I have shared here and the time spent together in this book.

I want to hear how you are getting on, or what you are struggling with, as it will help me understand and further develop this new area of social media I find myself in.

And I will share with you the people and ideas that can help us navigate these times and these digital waters we swim in.

Social Media For A New Age.

A co-creative digital self care comm-unity.

If you have any digital self-care and wellbeing strategies that help you and you would like to share them with me and my comm-unity, please tag me or use #socialmediaforanewage and I distribute with full credit.

*In every community, there
is work to be done.
In every nation, there
are wounds to heal.
In every heart, there is
the power to do it.*

Source: Good Reads;
Quote by Marianne Williamson

(Running for Presidency, 2020)

# #SOCIALMEDIAFORANEWAGE

# A Social Media Angel Self-Care Guide

There are many ways we can handle our individual and collective social media self-care from a more conscious standpoint. What follows are some of my favourite methods. Let me know what resonates with you or if you have any ideas to add to this list.

## *Having a Strategy of Love, Love, Love.*

Loving your platforms, loving your content, loving what you have to share, loving the people you have to share it with, bundled up with a big fat dose of love for yourself.

If you are not feeling the love, listen to this as a sign to take a break or get some help, or both, depending on where you are in your social media journey.

Check in with yourself and listen to your heart to tell you what you need to have a healthy and vibrant digital experience.

## *Take Your Own Sweet Time About It.*

Trusting in divine timing

And higher timelines

For your social media journey.

Taking breaks when you need to.

Hours, days, weeks, months as required.

Releasing the need for more numbers, for more followers, for doing what everyone else is doing.

Taking time to connect and communicate more effectively with who is already there, listening to or talking with you.

Stopping to think how we are using these digital means- email, messenger, Whatsapp, Instagram, LinkedIn, et al- to communicate effectively.

Pausing social media for a moment while taking time to re-strategise and *switch things up.* Trust that the people who matter will be there when you get back online. Maybe you will notice more of the people who are there, in front of you, when you do.

Learning more about what tools are available outside of Facebook.

Not being afraid to start somewhere anew.

Choosing a few key things to do and making those work for you.

Cutting back on how many platforms and accounts you are managing, or think you have to manage, or the amount of content you are making (this one is for the over-deliverers amongst us).

*Brendon, you suck at social media.
I hear it plenty.
But you have to understand people will
always tell you that what you're doing is
\*insufficient.\* They say all these things
I'm \*not\* doing that would make me
more 'popular' or 'viral'.
YES, we can always do more things
to fit in or be more popular, but
sometimes that is the path to an
inauthentic or forced life.
You gotta do you in YOUR style in a
way that makes you creatively happy.
Don't let them tell you that your
approach isn't working if you're happy.
Do your thing. I like my thing.*

Source: Instagram; Brendon Burchard @
brendonburchard

via Brooke Slick @brooke.slick -
thank you Brooke for sharing this with me.

# #SOCIALMEDIAFORANEWAGE

## *Co-creating All the Way.*

This book has come together as a co-creation, with things I have seen on social media and the mainstream media, quotes and stories weaving their way into the book in the most timely of fashions. Social media was mirroring, reflecting and speaking to me... helping me by giving examples to share.

I don't think we fully perceive as yet just how much we are co-creating, sharing ideas and concepts as they spread faster, energetically weaving in the digital field.

Social media can also bring out our inner narcissist sometimes (or at least it can with me!)

*Making social media not all about me.*
*How many people are following me,*
*Watching me, listening to me or responding to me.*
*Not me, me, me, see?*

I want to see us opening up the communication, learning from and with each other, sharing other people's voices, connecting and conversing, free from a hierarchy based on the number of Likes or Follows.

*Social Media For A New Age* in action.

As part of a personal commitment to co-creation on social media, *Inner Unicorn Question Time* is a video series for IGTV where I ask friends and connections in my life to answer some self care questions about social media.

If you would like to send me a video, let me know, as I would love to hear your voice, to share more about this important topic that involves all of us who use social media, particularly for our businesses.

It has been a beautiful way to increase connection, building on those relationships and gaining a better understanding of their social media lives, ethics, perspectives and digital wellbeing.

## *Communicating More Consciously.*

Creating committed time and space for connection, contact, comments and DMs rather than being so ad hoc and reactive is something I would like to be better at. I plan to do this by:

Making communication more proactive and meaningful.

Creating opportunities to speak and connect more deeply and personally.

Sending more voice notes so people can hear and feel rather than just read. I love receiving voice notes. (They can often be quicker to do too.)

If you want to join me in creating communication that unites us, here are some ideas:

Try asking those you are connected to if they have podcasts. Offer to speak on theirs, or see if they would like to co-create by speaking on yours (or on a live etc.)

Reach out to a few different people you feel drawn to and see what happens.

Enjoy the moments of connection you exchange in the form of emails, DMs and voice memos.

Feel into the synergy and how your energies connect and what they will do together in creative collaboration and comm-unication.

You never know where this may lead. New friends. New collaborations and creations. You may go from being a guest on someone's podcast to creating a retreat together. Creating beautiful bonds of friendship, support across the planet and connecting the web of light workers and light work in so many magical ways.

Visit profiles, reach out and connect to people you admire. Say hi to new followers, Likers, lookers, by looking at who and what energies are connecting into your digital space, your energy field.

Have clear intentions for your posts. In my first book I share a process called *The Four Intentions*, by my awesome friend, coach Helena Holrick. By using something like *The Four Intentions* (and you can find a podcast on iTunes where we share this process with you), you can create so much more clarity in what you create and in what you post. This creates a very different frequency to something which is being posted for 'the sake of it'.

Focus on how you are using social media as tool to connect and communicate in the best way with others who are on your frequency, others that you want to reach and meet.

Reducing the noise levels.

And the attention-grabbers.

And the anxiety.

Make it count.

Supporting one another in our online comm-unities, rather than feeling the veil of competition through the gamification, that was programmed into the system.

## *Being Aware*

We must become more aware of the information we consume.

Practising due diligence to find out if what we are reading or seeing is real, authentic and genuine- or if instead if it could be fake, manipulative or persuasive- this would serve us really well as we move through this next decade.

We can start by being more discerning when looking at articles and posts online, getting better at asking where the information is coming from, questioning its authority and intention both when reading it and when sharing it.

Also by listening to what our body tells us about what content feels good, we can identify who feels legit, inspiring, informative and kind, rather than just basing our opinions on the sales or Likes trail.

Looking at what platforms feel good for us to use. Taking time to explore other options and avenues outside of Facebook Inc.

Feeling into which feel ones might be having a negative impact on our overall wellbeing, which are just wasting our time… and which ones help us with our mission- and the ones that help us may very well be owned by Facebook!

Adjust accordingly.

Cultivate the ability to be able to tune into what content or people are of integrity, truth and alignment.

## *Watching What We Say.*

What you share = data. This data is then shared with companies, advertisers and governments (if they ask for it.)

Want less ads to know what is going on inside your head? Think about what you are sharing when you are on social media, from Messenger and DMs to comments, clicks, Amazon purchases and status updates. It all helps them know what might interest you. Personalisation can be cool but sometimes it is creepy. I do still think they are listening to my conversations and even to my thoughts sometimes! The ads are so accurate. In almost every interview I do we end up talking about this, as it happens to everyone.

We all have a story to tell about the time a Facebook advert seemed to know about a private conversation or appeared to just be plain psychic.

According to the big networks, they are not actually listening to what we say, but the data is. They have so many 'data points' that it apparently knows us better than we know ourselves.

Sometimes this is great - other times it does feel invasive.

But it isn't just watching what we say in case Big Brother is listening.

It is *also* about watching *what we say* when we send an email, a DM, or a comment...

Because we don't know if someone is having a bad day.

We don't know how we are being received on the other side of the screen.

We can be master misinterpreters through digital communication; not always seeing the context or hearing the tone correctly can cause all kinds of miscommunication.

*Be approximately 30% nicer online than you are in real life to allow for the potential misinterpretations of un-nuanced written text. Don't make people's days worse…*

Source: FutureLearn; Digital Wellbeing course from The University of York.

Taken from an article by Ned Potter.

# #SOCIALMEDIAFORANEWAGE

## *Cleaning Up our Timelines*

I have started to look at cleaning up my timelines in the same way I look at cleaning my kitchen: the more I use my kitchen, the more it needs cleaning .

If I am cooking up content and connections, I need to keep my counter and utensils clean otherwise I might get some bacteria or bugs or the mess will pile up and it will stress me out.

Keeping an eye on our digital counter tops is essential to maintaining a healthy digital diet.

Checking to see what is lurking at the back of our digital cupboards and throwing stuff out when it gets old and before it gets mouldy.

Unsubscribing from groups, accounts, emails and people that we no longer have interest in or digital time or resonance for if they are creating distraction or dissidence in your field.

Realising when things are taking up space without our awareness.

Cleaning up the things that no longer serve us in our digital timelines.

Having the freedom and permission to mute or unfollow at will.

## *Frequency of our Posts*

It is not just the content itself that holds our frequency, through our words, images, videos, podcasts and voice notes.

If we are being 30% nicer and kinder, this upgrades the energy and frequency of our social media vibration and output into the digital world. When our content impacts another human somewhere across the planet or down the road, this extra 30% can filter back into our embodied world, and into the planet.

Frequencies weaving through cyber space into physical space and into each other.

We can use social media to upgrade the frequency of the planet when we choose to use it to upgrade the frequency of each other.

So watch your frequency each time you post.

Are you posting out of FEAR- fear of not enough Likes, not being seen, not making the business work, not being liked, not being connected, out of FOMO- or am I posting out of LOVE- love for what is ready to share, love of sharing, love of what you share and love for those who receive it?

Remember that the timeline frequency- how *often* we post- can also have an impact on our digital wellbeing.

It can overwhelm our audience, our energetic receivers; if we post too much, those dialled into our frequency can feel overwhelmed if we post too often.

We should aim for *quality*, not *quantity*.

This works the other way round too; if I post a lot, I check and pick up my phone more. Balancing and adapting a slower frequency, how often I post doesn't feed my addictive tendencies.

If we collectively slowed down the pace of how much we post, the algorithms will have to adapt to us, not us to them.

It is symbiotic. We are more in control than we know.

## *Like it or Lump it.*

Likes provide a little dopamine hit.

Start noticing how much Likes affect you.

How it feels in your body when you are looking for and receiving Likes and comments.

Just as the negative to positive 4:1 ratio mentioned by Dr Phil Parker, I started to notice how much I was subconsciously feeling a low level of disappointment that not more people were liking posts, and noticing the people that did not, versus the people who did. It was subtle, but much like when I woke up thinking about the one negative Amazon review I received rather than the thirty-plus five star reviews, I was thinking about who wasn't liking and commenting rather than who was appreciating my work. And then on some level, I was feeling a sense of 'not good enough'.

I started to switch this around and really see who was there connecting with me in my digital spaces, appreciating and valuing their support and letting myself feel that sense connection. The thing we all want, rather than a self-imposed sense of disconnection and lack.

Begin by really looking, receiving and valuing those who have liked commented, shared your posts, those who love on you, whether it's a few or a few hundred or few thousand.

Really see those people who have made time to connect with you by making time to connect with them.

Turn Likes into a really good thing.

Become a connector.

Not a competitor.

Hiding Likes from public view should help with this.

## *Detoxing your Digital Time.*

A digital detox could be a day, a week or a month or more. You have to listen to what feels best for you. The *social media vortex of doom* is what I call that feeling when you know that social media is affecting your wellbeing.

*When you feel anxious,*
*overwhelmed and stressed out,*
*When it's too much to handle,*
*And you want to hide, not hang out.*
*You have entered the social media vortex of doom,*
*Where nothing works, and nothing blooms.*
*So take a break, put your phone down,*
*Switch airplane mode on,*
*Relax and chill out.*

Having this term for it really helps me if I notice I am spiralling from being online too much. If you notice that it is triggering anxiety or depression in anyway, call it out and take a break from it for a while. Trust me, it can really help. One of my social media buddies, Esther, posted something about this and I asked her if I could share it with you because it is very honest and I feel it will speak to some of you.

*Taking a month off FB. So here's a hard truth.*
*Right now I am a pretty crappy combination*
*of a low level of anxiety at all times mixed*

with mega-balls depressed. I'm taking some action and listening to my body. Which means unfortunately I need to take a break from Facebook.

I don't have a great relationship with social media. I find it overwhelming, a creative drain and a constant wheel of comparison and competition. I'm awful at responding to people and staying connected, because as soon as I log on I feel physically sick from the energy I pick up from the whole thing.

This needs to change because A.) Facebook is an amazing tool for staying in touch with people you love and B.) Facebook could be fantastic for business if I change my energy and relationship with it. But I've been feeling a nudge to take a break and have a social media detox and now I know I NEED to. I'm going to try and swap real life details with a few peeps I'm hoping to collaborate with, and others I want to stay connected with for the month.

There are two courses I'm taking that involve being part of private FB groups that I'll check once a week. But the reality is even though I've convinced myself taking a break will be difficult and stop me from taking advantage *of opportunities I'm so useless atm I'm missing them anyway!*

*Everything else can wait. I need to take some time to hopefully be creative away from social media and look after myself. I'll be spending today getting in touch with a few peeps about swapping emails/phone numbers and generally sorting my crap out. I'm not deactivating but will be deleting messenger from my phone and logging out for about a month.*

*Love you all! May your emotional, spiritual and practical energy reserves remain high!*

Source: Facebook; Esther De La Forde.

If you do not need to take a full detox like Esther, look instead at ways to switch off and close up like a shop or office does by 6pm each day. Try meeting up with people, working out, reading, making art or music, finding something creative or entertaining to do away from screens and devices instead.

## *Social Media-Free Sundays For All?*

And speaking of taking a break how about Social Media-Free Sundays for all? It is already a hashtag and practice that we are collectively playing with. My thoughts are that if everyone on social media were to go quiet and be offline on a Sunday, then no posting equals nothing to look at too.

It makes me think of Nyepi, the Balinese new year, where no-one can use electricity or cars for 24 hours. If millions of people stop for one day a week, it will make a difference to the amount of online traffic on Sundays.

A proper day off every week.

Keeping each other accountable.

Good for the planet too. Social media takes processing power which equals energy. I learned this while taking part in a debate I hosted on *Social Media For A New Age* at the Campfire Convention Campout. It's not something I had considered before, so taking a device-free, social media-free day once a week *en masse* could not only help manage the overwhelm of social media but also help the planet too!

*'Tsunami of data' could consume one fifth of global electricity by 2025. Billions of internet-connected devices could produce 3.5% of global emissions within 10 years and 14% by 2040, according to new research, reports Climate Home News.*

Source: The Guardian; *'Tsunami of data' could consume one fifth of global electricity by 2025.*

# *Being OK with Being Bored.*

Creating space to be bored.

Embracing it.

Allowing it.

Being it.

*'When we are free from stimulation that distracts us, we are brought to the end of our hiding and into new spaces of exploration,' Dodgen-Magee explains. 'When we have nothing to look at, listen to, or engage with, we are given the opportunity to see what we ourselves are made of, and unoccupied time can spark creativity and insight.'*

Source: Elite Daily; *4 Legit Benefits Of Boredom That'll Probably Surprise The Heck Out Of You,* BY <u>GEORGINA BERBARI</u> feat. Dr. Doreen Dodgen-Magee.

# #SOCIALMEDIAFORANEWAGE

## *Freedom in Your Framework to Flow Within*

Social media is not the be-all and end-all of business communications. I say this as much to myself as to you, as it can be easy to fall back on and hide behind a screen for all your networking needs.

The combined effect of good social media content, with good word of mouth, with direct contact alongside recommendations and referrals is what I see creating the best flow. Especially for those having well balanced digital wellbeing in their businesses and lives.

Social media can support the growth of your trajectory with an intentional, authentic communication framework, plan or strategy.

We don't all need to be 'Influencers' with tens of thousands of followers to succeed in business or in life.

If your current content framework or posting plan feels constricting, too full of things to do, create, edit and post… Notice this.

Do the process I recommended earlier from my friend Ryan…

*I got really quiet this morning. I put one hand on my chest and one hand on my belly, and said to myself 'I am here, I am listening. What do you want me to know?'*

If it does feel out of balance, give yourself some space and freedom within that framework, so that you can continue to deliver consistently, to deliver something you enjoy creating and your audience enjoys receiving.

This year I decided on a content framework that included a mix of media (video, micro blog and others) every week. Soon I realised, after having had a long break from posting, that posting consistently in this way every week does not work for me anymore. I was unconsciously checking too much to see if my posts had Likes.

I was spending more time on the apps because of the time needed to post itself alongside responding to people's comments etc.

Instead I have decided to go away, focus on and enjoy creating content away from social media, like writing this book, and preparing the next series of *Inner Unicorn Question Time*. Rather than getting stuck in the trap of *what do I post today?* like many of us do.

I will prepare for seasons and series of work that I share on social media, so I am not caught up in the treadmill of thinking I have to post every day or so many times a week, like I have been taught to and helped others to do as well.

We feel we have to do this, and then feel guilty when we don't- especially when we see everyone else doing it. Or are told we have to because of the algorithms.

This is why everyone needs to declare when they go on a digital detox, rather than just doing it.

WE continue to create an *always-on* culture, when we contribute to it by *always being on it*.

I have decided to throw caution to the wind. I want to work in new ways to deliver content to social media and not be afraid of each season break.

## *Beautiful Boundaries*

Setting boundaries starts by monitoring our digital environments.

Seeing who is coming into our digital field as a way of witnessing our vibration by looking at who is magnetised into it.

Protecting it.

Having boundaries with your time and your energy both internally and externally. Not always responding to a message or comment as soon as you see it.

Scanning for what and who brings you joy, in that exchange.

Looking closely at what and who lights you up online.

How do you feel when you connect there?

## *Standing Up and Shaking That Butt*

Standing up more often. Not hunching. Releasing. Moving. Shaking. Stretching. Walking. Flowing. Dancing. Shaking that butt.

## *Embody at Any Given Opportunity*

Encourage each other to take time away from the computers and devices to relax and socialise together in embodied spaces.

Creating more opportunities to gather offline.

Create meet-ups, lunches, workshops, talks and walks.

Arranging to meet up for a coffee or a chat.

# Conscious Use: A Daily Practice

When you open up an app, mobile or device ask yourself...

*What I am doing here? Is my use of this app intentional?*

Pausing to take a deep breath, or a couple, each time you pick up or notice that you are online.

Using the breathe to become a mini meditation throughout the day.

Saying a little Mantra, like *So Hum* or *Om Namah Shivay,* the mantra for eternal joy like my friend Jen uses, or a little mantra you make up of your own.

Creating a moment of presence and consciousness. A new habit.

More deep breaths, more connection with the body.

Putting the phone back down, if you picked it up without intention.

This is a new practice I am just starting to do; hopefully it will help us to stop picking up the mobile and getting lost in the endless scroll of doom so easily.

*This practice was inspired by Deviced!, by Doreen Dodgen-Magee, Tom Evans, meditation teacher, & Ryan James, We Won't Die Wondering.*

# A Meditation to Connect With Your Digital Comm-unity

Take three deep breaths and relax your body.

Now imagine you are hanging out on social media- writing comments, sending DM's, making an Instagram story or creating content for your connections, friends and comm-unity.

You want to reach them, you want to connect with them…

Take another breath and imagine the light of your essence filling up your heart. That light, that glow… travels from your heart and up into your throat and throughout your whole body… lighting up every cell as it moves from your heart… Connecting with everything that you are doing… The light of your essence, the love in your heart, transfers itself into the posts you create, messages you send and comments you make.

Now imagine this light, the light of your essence, the light from your heart space connecting with your friends, with your clients, with your community through your posts or through your comments.

See a web of light, your light and their light connecting with each other and dancing together. And as you dance together in this space you are weaving a heart-based connection.

Each time you practise embodying your essence and your light, and sharing this consciously with others, you are creating caring and nourishing energetic bonds which over time attracts connection and comm-unity, both online and offline.

Take another breath. And say thank you for the time shared together in this metaphysical digital space.

Then come back and open your eyes. Wiggle your fingers and wiggle your bum.

*The audio version of this and other meditations I have created are available on patreon.com/ socialmediaforanewage*

# THE EPILOGUE

*This journey with you*
*My dear friends,*
*Of seeing social media*
*Through a new lens,*
*Is just the beginning*
*Of this clean up and cleanse.*
*So lets come together*
*And transcend,*
*The digital dimension,*
*To help earth ascend.*

This feels like the end of a workshop, after processing a whole range of emotions and energy. The person sat next to you is now your friend, even though when you arrived you were nervous about having to speak to someone new, and you may even feel like giving them a hug (Glastonbury style).

There has been a lot for us to process together, from Facebook's data and advertising policies and Mark Zuckerberg's pivotal role in digital society to our own relationship with social media, that dopamine hit and how it can impact our wellbeing and mental health. We have looked to the future of digital communication, to emerging technologies such as virtual reality and AI Instagram Influencers and I have shared some ideas on how to navigate the *social media vortex of doom* with a strategy of love and self-care.

I hope you have been able to develop some personal strategies to help with your own digital wellbeing in this next decade. It is up to each of us to decide how we grow with social media and deal with our digital codependency. It is a very individual and complex relationship we all face; how do we best balance our use of technology for the good of the self and society?

I would love to hear about your ideas, plans and actions for managing your digital self-care. I will leave my contact details on the last page, where you can message, email or find out more as my work organically unfolds.

Here is me, hugging you through these words, as I wish you a fond adieu.

All beautiful human beings trying our best to figure out life. I am sending you my love as we work together to create a more human-centric relationship to social media.

I'm going to finish simply with a poem from the first book. It is one I am often asked to read out to close an interview or workshop. My friend Lucy Anne Chard tells me it always gives her the tingles.

It is called *Social Media For A New Age...*

*If light is information*
*And we are in the age of information,*
*Then we are also in the age of light.*
*If love is light,*
*Then love is information,*
*Which means we are in the age of love.*
*If social media is a place*
*For us to share information,*
*It is a place for us to share our*
*light and our love.*
*When we share our information*
*(light and love)*
*Creatively and consciously,*
*We connect with*
*And create our comm-UNITY.*

# RECOMMENDED READING & RESOURCES.

*Deviced!* by Doreen Dodgen-Magee

*Social Media For A New Age* by me (if you haven't already)

*Digital Minimalism* by Cal Newport

*Life Scale* by Brian Solis

*Indistractable* by Nir Eyal

*The Trust Manifesto* by Damian Bradfield

*The Social Organism: A Radical Understanding of Social Media to Transform Your Business and Life* by Oliver Luckett, and Michael J Casey.

*Cognitive Surplus - Creativity and Generosity in a Connected Age* by Clay Shirky

*The Art of Soulful Persuasion* by Jason Harris

*Connecting The Dots - The Conscious Communications Guide for Heart-Centred Businesses* by Sarah Lloyd

*The Wonder of Unicorns* by Diana Cooper

*Work Your Light Oracle Cards* by Rebecca Campbell

*Sassy She Oracle Cards* by Lisa Lister

Rays of Light, Concentration & Sacred Space - *Elixir Vibratoire* sprays by Amalie Phaneuf www.larunche-terre-etoile.ca

*Digital Wellbeing* by The University of York for FutureLearn.

https://www.futurelearn.com/courses/digital-wellbeing/

*Social Media Ethics MOOC* by the University of Sydney

https://www.coursera.org/learn/ethical-social-media

Digital Awareness UK; Award-winning, leading digital wellbeing agency, promoting safe and responsible use of technology

https://www.digitalawarenessuk.com

Royal Society for Public Health; *Looking after your self-ie: A guide to finding your balance on and offline.*

https://www.rsph.org.uk/our-services/e-learning/courses/free-courses/looking-after-your-selfie.html

# BONUS CHAPTER

## Membership portals.

I was going to include this section in Chapter Four, *Predictions and Future Proofing*. As I was editing, the book felt a bit heavy and something needed trimming back. Although I know this will be interesting to a section of my audience and client base, I know it will not be as relevant to a lot of people reading the book. In it I get a bit geeky and into details about the trend towards membership sites, digital networks and communities, as a digital living room space outside of Facebook that can be monetised. I'm all for it - but I have some feedback from my investigations that I invite you to consider.

I am still tinkering with a format of this that will work for me. I have decided to recommit to Patreon as a way to do this, for those that want to receive it. I have seen that value is relative which inspires me to run it as a digital honesty box by letting you decide how much you want to pay for the additional content I create. It is $1 per month to enter this digital space of mine, from there you choose the value it has to you. You will receive your content via email and there is also a free app you can use too.

This Bonus Chapter will be on there.....

www.patreon.com/socialmediaforanewage

*Membership platforms are a popular option for creating a Living Room outside of Facebook, but it does not automatically make them a community, even if it says so in the marketing material. As part of this enquiry, I explored a number of membership and subscription-based platforms as a consumer: Patreon, Mighty Networks, Disciple, as well as Facebook's new subscription service. I signed up to and joined a number of well-known content creators, spiritual teachers, astrologers and business leaders. Genuinely interested in their content, looking at how it all made me feel and how I interacted with these platforms, people, communities and models. This is my experience... Take from it what you will....*

# ACKNOWLEDGEMENTS

A massive high-five to myself for following the intuition and just getting on with it. It has been pretty amazing going from thinking I was not going to write this one, to having it written in one moon cycle and released by the next.

My heart, my gut and my guides. The fairies and my Unicorn friends, and the writing guide that showed up in my right ear and was taking over the keyboard on occasion. To Crystal Cat for being keeper of the writing cave, delivering nuzzles, cuddles and purrs as I needed them.

All clients past, present, future. To Diana, Sue, Julia, Maja and everyone I have worked with this year, you inspire me to keep going. Always a co-creation.

To my mum and dad. You have both been amazing through some of the most challenging of times. So proud to be your daughter and to make you proud in return. Thanks always for believing, trusting and loving me x

To all my friends, online and offline, thank you. Kat for the gift of friendship to family, it means the world to me. Bea, god daughter of dreams,

Unicorn love 4 ever. Henrietta & Harry; BFF's beyond words. Lisa, for all of it (inc. Westlife), love you. Huw, knighted, crowned... Whatever next? Jen for being cosmic you. Sarah, Erin, is it time for queso? Helena for this lifecycle (and the rest). Cari, for the VaBali Berlin upgrades. To my Ko Phangan peeps, to Gracie & our beach walks. To Sunset Hill, Moo and Jenny, Khob Khun Ka for your love and kindness. <3 To the Glastonbury crew, and Jade, Keith & Joseph. Natty, Ryan, Morgan and CK big love too. Jdot, miss you.

To the team: Sean, for publishing. Jesse for being the best, most magical fairy editor/ proof reader just at the moment I needed it. Huw for helping with cover design ideas and Peter for design, prepping and uploading. Dani for illustrations. To the feedback team for honest opinions and feels.

THANK YOU.

# ABOUT KATIE
# AKA KDOT,
# SOCIAL MEDIA ANGEL

Known to my clients as their Social Media Angel, I have been working in social media since the MySpace days. My highlights include winning a Gold *Sony Radio Academy Award* for the first ever "Best Internet Programme Award", setting up social media agency Kdot in 2007 and growing a small London-based team to help a range of clients from pop-stars to publishers, at a time when social media was still in its infancy.

An interest and need for de-stressing took on me retreat to Italy in 2011 with John Parkin and his wife Gaia, authors of *F\*\*k It; The Ultimate Spiritual Way...* This ultimately led me to Hay House UK, where they saw my talent for social media trends and ideas, hiring me to help them build their digital presence and manage their platforms. Thanks to them, I've worked with some bestselling authors and experts in the field of wellbeing, mind, body and spirit.

Moving away from agency life and going solo as a consultant in 2014, I continued to manage platforms for Hay House authors, coaching 1-2-1 and beginning to deliver workshops and talks. I published my first book in 2018; a self published hybrid deal with *That Guys House,* wanting to move quickly due to the fast paced nature of social media. *Social Media For A New Age* went on to be shortlisted as a finalist in the UK's *Business Book Awards* in Self Development; it also won a Janey Loves *Platinum Award* and made the finals, being highly commended in the *Wishing Shelf Independent Book Awards,* and it has received lots of lovely 5\* reviews on Amazon.

The media are showing some interest, with recent features in a number of different publications including *Thrive Global, Health and Fitness* and *Soul & Spirit Magazine.*

Moving into social media and marketing ethics, how we use it more carefully and effectively, without burnout. I'm focused on supporting people with their digital self-care, within business and the different ways we use social media.

# CONTACT, CONNECT & COLLABORATE.

I would love to hear from you

Here are some of the best ways to get in touch directly:

Connect, comment, DM or email me on Instagram @katiekdot_socialmediangel instagram.com/katiekdot_socialmediaangel

There is an email contact form at the bottom of the homepage on socialmediaforanewage.com

Support my work, say hi and get additional content through Patreon

patreon.com/socialmediaforanewage

If you are interested in working with me, as a coach / consultant on using Social Media in a New Age way and would like to find out more about working one to one, or having me speak with your team or organisation, please get in touch.

I am always interested in being interviewed on podcasts, live chats and pre-records for channels and membership sites; message me if you would like to propose something.

If you would like to collaborate by having me at speak at one of your events, workshops or retreats to talk and share about Social Media For A New Age, I am open to invites and offers.

I will try to create some more in-person events, be it collaborations or solo.

Keep a look out for those on socialmediaforanewage.com

Made in the USA
Coppell, TX
28 October 2020

40384392R00118